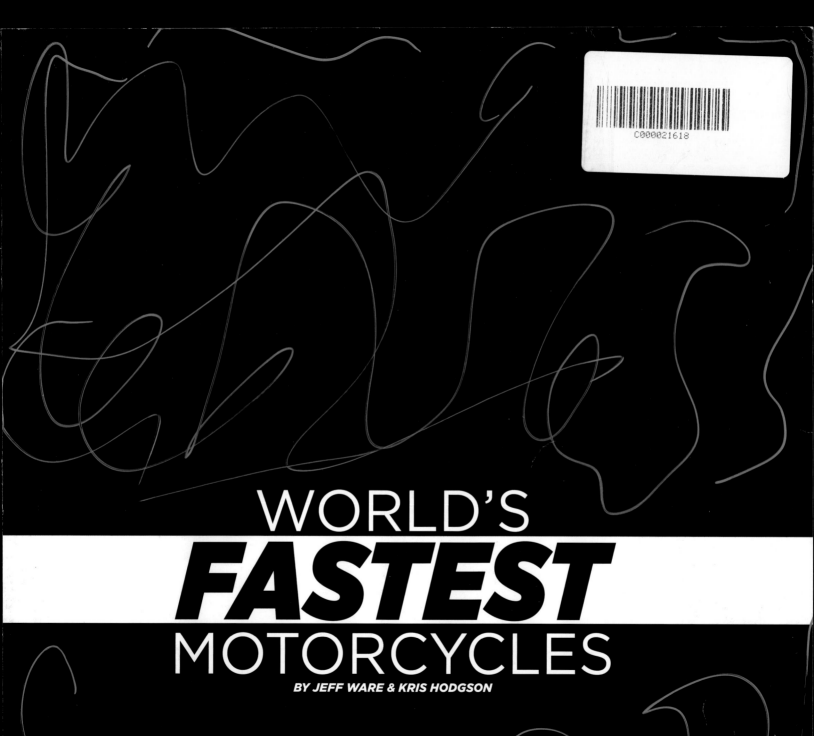

WORLD'S
FASTEST
MOTORCYCLES
BY JEFF WARE & KRIS HODGSON

The Ducati Superleggera was produced as a limited run with just 500 available, featuring titanium, magnesium and carbon-fibre compomnents to keep weight down, as well as Ohlins FL916 forks, a TTX shock and a dry weight of just 155kg.

Kawasaki's H2R boasts a supercharged engine with similarities
to the ZX-10R but producing over 300hp, created with the help
of Kawasaki Heavy Industries company collaboration.

The MV Agusta F4 RR is the brand's flagship model, featuring
a trellis frame, single sided swingarm, Ohlins suspension with a
full Brembo braking package, and boasting 201hp.

INTRODUCTION

Welcome to *World's Fastest Motorcycles*, where we celebrate the power and speed of the fastest accelerating, highest top speed and completely street legal motorcycles on the planet.

These are the bikes that you and I can buy and ride off the showroom floor, not bikes that are limited to MotoGP or World Superbike teams. Some of these exotic machines are incredibly expensive, making them rare and exclusive, while some are affordable and top selling.

What they all have in common, however, is blinding acceleration and speed. They are the Supercars of the motorcycle world. They are Superbikes...

Choosing the bikes was difficult as there are so many fantastic machines – however, these are my pick for the most iconic or pure performance levels out of the lot. I also took into account the styling of the bikes and the overall package – but mostly, just the speed...

We have showcased the best of the best – the incredible 300hp H2R and H2 street version are futuristic machines that absolutely blew the world away on release.

Kawasaki built these machines with one thing in mind. Acceleration. They have completely re-written the rulebooks with the supercharged 340km/h beast that only a lucky few own, including a dozen or so in Australia.

Before the H2 came along the King of the roads was the mighty Suzuki Hayabusa. When it arrived in 1999 it was the first production bike capable of over 300km/h.

Subsequent models have been limited to 299km/h in a 'gentleman's' agreement between manufacturers, a handshake rule that has been broken by a few over the years including Kawasaki and MV, the latter with the stunning F4 312 RR, the name saying it all – a claimed top speed of 312km/h.

The Kawasaki ZX14 is Kawasaki's answer to the Hayabusa.

It's a 1400cc, big, bad, high-speed aerodynamic machine built purely to go fast on. The ZX has a horsepower advantage over the Suzuki but an acceleration disadvantage. Both bikes are the fastest out there and leave the litre-class bikes behind...

If you want a MotoGP bike for the street you have one real deal choice – the rare and raw Ducati Desmosedici RR. Launched back in 2006/2007, the Desmo was as close to Casey Stoner's MotoGP bike as any machine has ever been to the real thing. In fact, it was basically a MotoGP bike with lights and rego.

At over $100k a pop the bike was for the rich and plenty were crashed. But still, to me, this is the world's wildest street bike hands down.

The Yamaha VMAX came out in the mid 1980s and was the fastest acceleration mass production motorcycle at the time. In 2008 Yamaha re-released the bike and again, took the trophy for what is still the fastest accelerating motorcycle on our streets. Once you ride a VMAX flat out from 0 – 150km/h, nothing gives you the same thrill again...

Of course a book celebrating the fastest bikes in the world would not be complete without the BMW HP4, Yamaha YZF-R1, Kawasaki ZX-10R, Honda CBR1000RR Fireblade, EBR 1190RX, KTM RC8R or Aprilia RSV4.

For the super exclusive, we have included perhaps the ultimate Ducati superbike – the stunning Superleggera.

Enjoy the technical breakdown on each bike, along with full factory specifications and a ride impression. **– JEFF WARE**

Aprilia's RSV4 RF is a limited 500 unit production of the new RSV4, with Superpole colours, the full Race Pack and a numbered tope yoke.

28

40

52

64

74

82

CONTENTS

10 INTRODUCTION

16 WHERE IT ALL STARTED:
THE NEED FOR SPEED

THE MACHINES

28 KAWASAKI H2 AND H2R

40 SUZUKI HAYABUSA

52 KAWASAKI ZX-14R

64 DUCATI DESMOSEDICI RR

74 MV AGUSTA F4 312 RR

82 YAMAHA VMAX

90 APRILIA RSV4

98 YAMAHA YZF-R1

106 SUZUKI GSX-R1000

114 KAWASAKI ZX-10R

122 HONDA CBR1000RR

130 DUCATI SUPERLEGERRA

138 EBR 1190RX

146 BMW HP4

154 KTM RC8R

GENERAL ENQUIRIES Universal Magazines 1300 303 414
MANAGING EDITOR Jeff Ware
EDITOR Kris Hodgson
EDITORIAL ASSISTANT Heather Ware
CONTRIBUTORS Roland Brown, Tony Wilding, Warwick Maguire, James Pralija, Keith Muir
DESIGNER Michael Ohanesian
UNIVERSAL MAGAZINES CHAIRMAN/CEO Prema Perera
PUBLISHER Janice Williams **CHIEF FINANCIAL OFFICER**
Vicky Mahadeva **ASSOCIATE PUBLISHER** Emma Perera
ASSOCIATE PUBLISHER Karen Day **CIRCULATION DIRECTOR**
Mark Darton **CREATIVE DIRECTOR** Kate Podger **EDITORIAL**
PRODUCTION MANAGER Anastasia Casey **PREPRESS MANAGER** Ivan
Fitz-Gerald **MARKETING & ACQUISITIONS MANAGER** Chelsea Peters

 90

 98

 106

 114

 122

 130

138

146

154  15

EARLY PIONEERS

THE Turbo ERA

SUPERBIKES

★ FOR ★

the street

Electronics

AND

HIGH HORSEPOWER

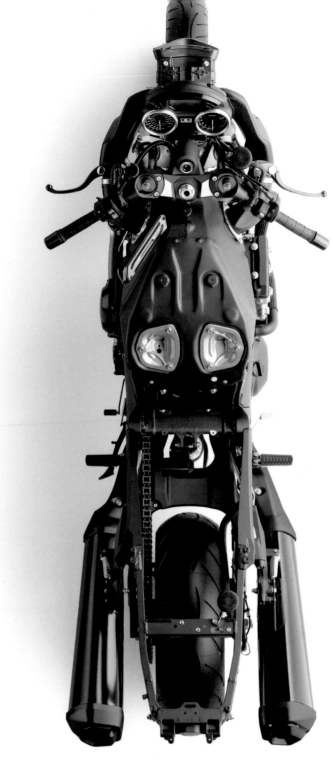

FUTURISTIC
FANTASIES
BECOME REALITY

The Hayabusa remains a favourite among drag racers, custom bike builders and tourers alike, covering a variety of riders and niches not seen with most other motorcycles...

KAWASAKI NINJA H2

A SUPERCHARGED 357KM/H ALIEN LOOKING MOTOGP-LIKE ACCELERATING BIKE? MEET THE NINJA...

CHASSIS

The tubular steel frame shared by both H2 Ninjas is unlike anything that Kawasaki has built before. The steel tubes are of differing dimensions, laser cut to ensure accuracy, partially hand-welded and finished in metalflake Kawasaki green.

The firm says this frame design was chosen, instead of the familiar aluminium beam layout, because it allows a little flex, which improves stability at very high speed. The layout also allows engine heat to escape and gives room for the H2's single air duct from the fairing nose and the H2R's similar carbon-fibre duct on each side of the bike.

The rear sub-frame is aluminium, as is the single-sided swing-arm, chosen to allow room on the right side for the exhaust's silencer – which in the case of the standard H2 is a large and ugly device that the UK importer, for one, is replacing with a more attractive and tuneful carbon-fibre Akrapovic can. (The H2R's megaphone racepipe will require quietening even for track days.)

Inevitably the Ninja H2 is heavier than a conventional superbike, with a kerb weight of 238kg (to the H2R's 216kg), but it gives away nothing at all in trickness.

There's no skimping with the top shelf parts, which are shared by both models. Suspension is by KYB, including 43mm forks with Air-Oil Separate cartridges, developed in motocross. Brakes are a blend of 330mm discs and Brembo radial calipers, with a revised version of the ZX-10R's race ABS.

It initially seemed slightly far-fetched when Kawasaki named their new supercharged bikes the Ninja H2 and H2R, after the notoriously quick and scary 750cc two-stroke triples of the early '70s. After all, the new 998cc fours were hugely powerful but surely, like all modern superbikes, they'd be honed to a flawless level of controllability and crammed with electronics that made them easy to ride even for a relative novice?

That's not what I'm thinking as I brake the H2 to a halt outside a Losail circuit pit box at the end of a session, climb off and stagger into the garage with eyes wide,

heart pounding and a broad but slightly relieved grin beneath my visor. If there's any streetbike that deserves to be named after that famously quick and crazy H2 triple, it's this far more rapid blown Kawasaki, with its 207bhp output and brutal throttle response.

And as for the H2R... The original bike of that name was a factory racing triple whose evil handling earned it the nickname, 'Green Meanie'. But fast and furious as that H2R was, it couldn't even approach the acceleration of its extraordinary 2015 namesake, which produces no less than 319bhp and left my ears ringing as it screamed down the Qatari circuit's pit

straight, recording a maximum of 319km/h on its digital speedometer (one rider managed 322km/h) before I interrupted its seemingly limitless acceleration by braking for the next bend.

These supercharged Ninjas look different to any other bikes and their characters are even more extraordinary. The single-seat H2 roadster, which getting onto costs twice as much as Kawasaki's ZX-10R, seems the tiniest bit sensible only by the standards of its even more outrageous sibling, which is almost twice as expensive, not street legal and has an exhaust so loud that in many countries the H2R won't be allowed even on track days.

Kawasaki are happy to admit that both were developed partly in an attempt to regenerate the sense of excitement that surrounded those wild, marque-defining machines of the early '70s. And also to emphasise the corporate strength of a giant corporation that called on several divisions, including its aerospace branch, to contribute to the project.

The results are undeniably spectacular, especially with the H2R whose carbon-fibre bodywork incorporates large fins designed to provide downforce at ultra-high speed. Even the H2 looks like nothing else on the road, with its complex shapes and shimmering mirror-finish paintwork, which is applied by hand and contains a layer of real silver.

The 998cc, 16-valve engine shares dimensions with the ZX-10R but Kawasaki emphasise that it's all new and that the motor and supercharger were purpose designed to suit each other. Features include composite Inconel/steel valves, lower compression ratio, cast rather than forged pistons (to withstand heat) and a new MotoGP-derived gearbox. Despite their power outputs the two motors are very similar, differing mainly in their camshafts. The supercharger feeds a rigid aluminium airbox, and turns at 9.2 times crank speed – so at up to 130,000rpm in the H2R.

Kawasaki's first steel trellis frame was chosen because at very high speed it allows a bit of flex, which the development team found was beneficial for stability. Suspension by KYB is conventional and of high quality, with adjusters on the fork tops protruding through the immaculately machined top yoke. The riding position is more relaxed than the ZX-10R's, with handlebars 10mm higher and wider, footrests slightly further forward and a roomy, generously padded seat that is horizontally adjustable and shaped to give support under acceleration.

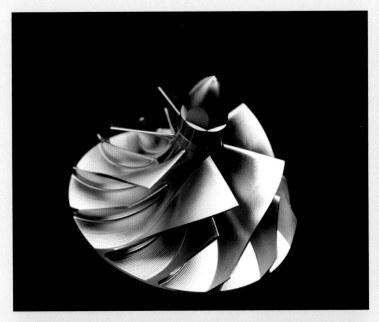

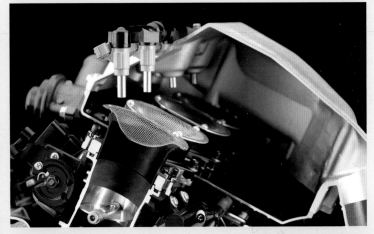

ENGINE

The basic 998cc, 16-valve powerplant is all new, not a revamped ZX-10R unit, despite the obvious similarities and identical dimensions of 76 x 55mm. Supercharged engines like these generate a lot of heat and put huge demand on parts such as bearings, so the H2 lump was designed to put up with up to twice as much stress as a conventionally aspirated engine. Pistons are cast, rather than forged, to cope better with very high temperatures, and have flat tops to reduce compression from the ZX-10R's 13:1 to under 9:1.

The all-important supercharger was designed specifically for this job at specialist divisions within the huge Kawasaki group of companies. It turns at 9.2 times the speed of the crankshaft, so at the H2R's maximum of 14,000rpm it's spinning at roughly 130,000rpm and cramming lots of mixture

into the engine's combustion chambers. It's located behind the cylinders, generates 2.4 times atmospheric pressure and feeds a rigid aluminium airbox.

To withstand the extreme heat of the supercharged combustion the exhaust valves are made from two materials, Inconel and steel, that are friction-welded together at their centres.

The two engines are very similar, the only differences being the camshafts, head gaskets and clutch. But their outputs are very different, the standard H2 makes 197bhp (200PS) at 11000rpm, or 207bhp with ram-air, the H2R puts out a staggering 319bhp (326PS) when ram-air is taken into account. Kawasaki insist that the H2 can't be converted to H2R specification, though that might not prevent people trying.

STYLING

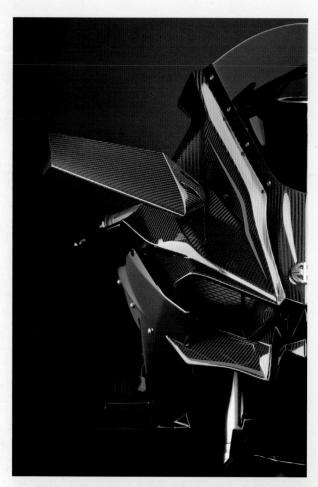

As speed increases, wind resistance increases exponentially and to be able to operate in the ultra-high speed range, a combination of high power and slippery aerodynamics was needed for the H2R. With power requirements taken care of by the supercharged engine, the next step was to design bodywork that both minimised drag and added control when riding at ultra-high speed. Assistance from Kawasaki's Aerospace Company was enlisted in creating the aerodynamically sculpted bodywork to ensure maximum aerodynamic efficiency.

When viewed from the side, the Ninja H2R does not seem to have the aggressive forward-canted stance of most modern supersport models as such a posture would create drag that would hinder top speed. Instead, the stance is very neutral, almost flat – like a Formula 1 car – to make the body as aerodynamically sleek as possible.

The aerodynamically shaped upper cowl uses lips and lines to help direct airflow over its surface, while the upper cowl positions the Ram Air

intakes in the most efficient position. The cowl itself is formed from lightweight CFRP and is designed to afford wind protection at ultra-high speed – its tall screen is designed to help create a wind-free pocket for the rider.

The compact side cowls were designed to assist with heat dissipation, while the rear cowl has an extremely compact three-piece design. The centre portion is taller, creating an aerodynamic form that helps smooth airflow as it passes the rider. Wind is also able to pass between the centre and side-pieces, reducing air resistance.

In place of mirrors, the Ninja H2R features CFRP wings mounted on the upper cowl. Designed by Kawasaki's Aerospace company, they feature winglets to help smooth airflow near the wingtip by reducing the strength of the wingtip vortices that would otherwise cause turbulence or disturb the laminar flow needed for the wings to effectively generate downforce.

Two-blade wings are also featured on the side cowls. These wings also feature winglets and further add to the downforce generated by the chin spoiler and upper wings. Design of the upper cowl incorporates a chin spoiler.

A star-pattern five-spoke wheel design were also developed based on analysis and testing to determine the optimum rigidity balance for ultra-high speed performance, with the analysis technology used in their development coming from World Superbike.

THE H2R'S WINGS ARE INTEGRAL FOR CREATING THE NECESSARY DOWNFORCE...

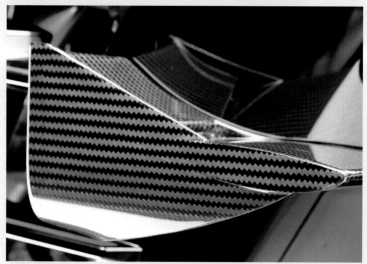

SATOAKI ICHI - PROJECT LEADER

"We heard a lot of customers, and also people inside Kawasaki, saying that nowadays motorcycle performance is getting better and better, the bikes are easier to control, but there is something missing – and that's the excitement of riding.

"At Kawasaki our core brand is performance and excitement, so we felt a strong need to develop something very special to satisfy those customers' feelings.

"The maximum horsepower of a (conventionally aspirated) bike was around 200bhp so we set the target at around 1.5 times that.

"We could have gone to 400bhp but then the engine

design got much heavier. We wanted to develop an enjoyable bike, so we decided to stop at around 300bhp.

"The H2 is not designed to cut every second on lap time. We wanted an enjoyable, high-performance sports bike. We targeted a customer who is experienced, maybe with a ZZR1400, so the age is relatively high. So we made the seat reasonably thick, and the handlebar position a little bit more upright to give a more comfortable riding position.

"Supercharging is one of the key technologies for Kawasaki. Being able to produce the supercharger in-house brings a lot of possibilities, so it's an important direction for the future."

SPECIFICATIONS

KAWASAKI NINJA H2 (H2R)

CLAIMED POWER:
147kW[200hp]@11000rpm, 207hp with ram-air)
(228kW[306hp])@14000rpm, 326hp with ram-air)

CLAIMED TORQUE:
133.5Nm@10500rpm
(165Nm@12500rpm)

CLAIMED WEIGHT: 238kg (216kg)

FUEL CAPACITY: 17L

ENGINE: Liquid-cooled, transverse-four, DOHC, 16-valves, 998cc, 76 x 55mm bore x stroke, 8.5:1 (8.3:1) compression ratio, four dual injection 50mm throttle bodies, Kawasaki supercharger, KTRC, KLCM, KEBC, QKS

GEARBOX: Six-speed with quick-shift

CLUTCH: Wet multi-plate slipper

CHASSIS: Laser cut, hand welded, tubular steel frame, aluminium rear sub-frame and single-sided swingarm, Rake: 24.5° (25.1°), Trail: 103mm (108mm)

SUSPENSION: 43mm KYB AOS-II USD forks, adjustable preload, compression and rebound damping, 120mm spring travel, KYB Uni-Trak mono-shock, adjustable preload, high and low-speed compression and rebound damping, 135mm wheel travel,

BRAKES: KIBS, dual 330mm front rotors, Brembo radial four-piston calipers, single rear 250mm rotor, twin-piston caliper

WHEELS & TYRES: Cast aluminium star-pattern five-spoke wheels, 120/70 x 17in, 200/55 x 17in, Bridgestone Battlax RS10FG (120/60 x 17in, 190/65 x 17in, Bridgestone V01F/R)

DIMENSIONS:

WHEELBASE: 1450mm

GROUND CLEARANCE: 130mm

SEAT HEIGHT: 825mm (830mm)

OVERALL HEIGHT: 1160mm

OVERALL LENGTH: 2070mm

OVERALL WIDTH: 770mm

INSTRUMENTS: Digital multi-function display, analogue tachometer

RIDE IMPRESSIONS

So at least I was sitting comfortably when I cautiously tweaked the throttle for the first time, in second gear – and the H2 jerked forward with a violence that immediately announced the bike's aggressive character. This didn't make the H2 remotely easy to ride but it sure did make it exciting, especially on a Losail track where I soon learned to dial in a touch of throttle before the apex of a bend, to avoid upsetting the angry bike mid-corner.

Then, when past the apex, winding it on further sent the Ninja scorching forward, while I held on tight and flicked through the box with the help of the efficient quick-shifter.

The adjustable traction control system helped keep the front wheel down, though I wasn't relying on it fully. The H2 charged so hard that it had just about reached its electronically limited 300km/h maximum by the end of the straight. Its only disappointment was the muted exhaust note, which left the most memorable sound the supercharger's twittering on a closed throttle. (H2s sold in some markets will be fitted with a more stylish and tuneful carbon-fibre Akrapovic can.)

Handling was very good, although not super-sport sharp because with a kerb weight of 238kg the H2 is notably heavier. Its relatively wide bars contributed to respectable agility, and Bridgestone slicks (as fitted to the H2R – the H2 will come with Battlax RS10FG street rubber) supplied reassuring levels of grip. Brembo radial calipers and 330mm discs

ensured powerful, fade-free stopping, though the ABS cut in earlier than the best systems.

As a rapid roadster the H2 should have plenty going for it, provided you're travelling light. (There's no pillion seat, and don't even think about risking that paint with a tank bag.) The 17-litre capacity will limit range but the H2's respectable wind protection, excellent ride quality, comprehensive instrument panel and clear mirrors will add to its appeal.

This Ninja is far from an ordinary bike, and its mirror finish paint will be a nightmare if chipped, but in some ways it should prove relatively normal to own. It has typical service intervals that should keep most owners going for ages and will come with a normal Kawasaki warranty. (By contrast the higher-revving H2R will come with no warranty at all and will require a service after every 15 hours' hard use.)

Despite that the Ninja H2 can't justify its high price on overall performance or all-round ability. This bike would make sense only if you could live with its abrupt power delivery and value its unmistakable look, immaculate detailing, unique supercharged technology, and most of all its ferocious, mind-altering acceleration.

It's far from a bike for every rider but it is a magical machine that was conceived to generate excitement and remind the world of Kawasaki's spirit – and which does exactly that.

H2R

Two things above all stand out about the H2R – its astonishing speed and its equally outrageous sound from a straight-through exhaust as the supercharged powerplant screamed out that 319bhp output and the Kawasaki stormed down the Losail straight at a rate that no production motorcycle could approach.

If I'd found the courage to get on the power a fraction earlier or harder out of the Losail circuit's final turn, I'd possibly have carried an extra couple of mph all down the straight, and seen the digital speedo record 200mph (322km/h) before I braked for the first turn.

Then again, the H2R's power delivery might just have been too much even for the traction control and the sticky rear Bridgestone slick – in which case I'd have been spat so high that I would hardly have needed an ambulance to join the German rider who'd high-sided himself to Doha hospital from this very spot the previous day.

In fact the H2R was memorably faster and louder but no harder to ride than the H2 and handled and braked even better thanks to its blend of near-identical

chassis and less weight. And in a way that hint of menace epitomises the appeal of the Ninja H2R. This bike is mad, bad and slightly dangerous – an antidote to the modern world of increasingly fast but high-tech, electronically controlled, safe and almost sensible superbikes.

It still seems barely believable that Kawasaki has released a bike that is far more powerful than any MotoGP racer, and is rumoured to have recorded a speed of 357km/h when geared-up and ridden on a test oval by a factory tester. Let's hope that at least some H2R owners actually find a location and the willingness to ride their bikes, because it would be a huge shame if machines as special as these are merely polished and displayed as unused investments or museum exhibits.

Kawasaki are possibly the only motorcycle manufacturer with the breadth of resources to develop the Ninja H2R, and almost certainly the only one that would have dared put such an extreme machine into production. And for that we should all be truly grateful.

– Roland Brown

SUZUKI
HAYABUSA
THE KING NAMED AFTER THE BLACKBIRD HUNTING PEREGRINE FALCON IN JAPAN...

For a standard, non-special edition motorcycle, Suzuki's Hayabusa is possibly one of the most iconic machines produced, with a part of its claim to fame being as the fastest production motorcycle for most of its life, a claim the manufacturer's top speed agreement protected.

The earliest models, from 1999 and 2000, were created prior to this restriction however and aren't limited, making them a popular collector's and aficionado's choice.

The first generation Hayabusa, the name for Peregrine Falcon in Japanese and a bird known for hunting Blackbirds, coincidentally, featured a 1299cc liquid-cooled in-line four-cylinder, with a bore and stroke of 81 x 63mm and a top speed of up to 312km/h on the unrestricted models.

Suspension was fully adjustable inverted telescopic forks, with a Link-type fully adjustable rear shock. Tokico six-piston calipers with 320mm rotors provided stopping power on the front, while the bike's styling was largely influenced by wind-tunnel testing, with designer Koji Yoshirua admitting the original Hayabusa was designed to turn heads.

THE LATEST GENERATION HAYABUSA GAINED FORGED PISTONS AND CRANK, TITANIUM VALVES AND POWER WAS BOOSTED TO 197HP AT THE CRANK...

and exhaust valve is 14.1 and 11.7 grams lighter respectively.

Valve angle remained 14 degrees and length and diameter are unchanged. The lighter valves allow for lighter valve springs, a single spring each valve compared to two on the previous model, higher lift decreased mechanical losses.

Valve lift increased from 8.8 to 9mm on the intake side and from 7.5 to 8.6mm on the exhaust side. The intake valves open at 43 degrees BTDC and close at 58 degrees ATDC, with 281 degrees duration, while exhaust timing is 62 degrees BTDC opening and close 24 degrees ATDC, giving 266 degrees duration. The cam chain tensioner is hydraulically operated and is the same as the unit fitted to the GSX-R750. The camshaft material remained unchanged.

The crankcases feature a reed valve to prevent pressure waves from the airbox.

There were also some gearbox changes. Fifth and sixth gearsets were widened to 18mm, and first and second narrowed to 18mm. An oilstream is constantly sprayed onto fourth, fifth and sixth gearsets to reduce mechanical noise and decrease gear wear.

The clutch features Suzuki's hydraulically controlled back-torque limiting system, which reduces pressure on the clutch pack on deceleration.

ENGINE

The Hayabusa engine remains unchanged however the last major update in 2008 was fairly big. Stroke was increased 2mm to give a capacity hike, while bore remained 81mm. The cylinders are coated with SCEM (Suzuki Composite Electro Chemical Material) to improve heat transfer and ring seal, and the U shaped cut outs at the bottom of each cylinder were enlarged, to help the air flow to the next cylinder on each downward stroke.

The pistons were an all-new forged three-ring slipper design, with cutaway sides and smaller 18mm diameter gudgeon pins, and

are five grams lighter per piston. The new shape of the piston crown contributes to the increase in compression from 11.0:1 to 12.5:1. The upper compression and oil control rings are coated with a chrome-nitride coating and the upper ring also has an L shaped cross section for improved sealing on the compression stroke.

The chrome-moly conrods are shot peened for additional strength and the forged crank got new crank pin positions and revised balance to create the longer stroke. Titanium valves replaced the old steel ones and each intake valve

EXTENSIVE WIND TUNNEL DEVELOPMENT ALLOWED THE HAYABUSA TO REACH ITS 312KM/H TOP SPEED, WITH THE EARLY GENERATION RESETTING THE BAR ON TOP SPEED.

The Hayabusa's unusual styling has carried through two generations of the bike with research during development of the second generation showing that despite having detractors the bike's looks had equally ardent supporters.

Part of the Hayabusa's success is no doubt that despite its massive maximum speed, impressive power and unusual looks, the bike is an extremely capable machine for a huge variety of riding uses, from touring, drag racing to just everyday use. Plus the Hayabusa is a very popular machine for custom bike projects of all types.

The second generation Hayabusa was released in 2008, with a raft of changes, particularly when you look at the performance on offer. Revisions of the head, pistons and exhaust boosted power to 197hp at the crank, or over 170hp at the rear wheel.

This also brought the new generation in line with noise and emission regulations, while helping keep the outlay put into these new bikes at a minimum.

Changes for the second generation included an additional 2mm of stroke, bringing capacity out to 1340cc, while compression was raised to 12.5:1. The cylinder head was revised, with lighter titanium valves, lighter pistons and with reed valves added to

CHASSIS & STYLING

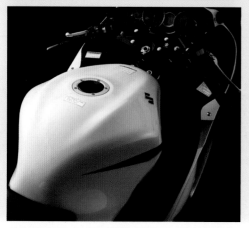

Suzuki spent plenty of time in the wind tunnel during development of the Hayabusa. The shape is designed to reduce drag, particularly from the rider's head, knees, elbows and shoulders. All fairing fasteners are hidden and the shape of the intakes and the top of the screen are also streamlined. The top of the tank is low to help with tucking down and the indicators and rear lights are integrated into the bodywork.

The frame is light thanks to the removal of unnecessary brackets and the wheelbase is 1480mm, while rake is 23.4 degrees and trail 93mm.

The 43mm KYB inverted forks feature a DLC (Diamond Like Coating) on the inner stanchions to reduce stiction and eliminate surface irregularities. The forks are fully adjustable and wheel travel is 120mm. A steering damper is also fitted to the lower triple-clamp.

The shock is a KYB unit and has a 14mm rod. The shock piston is 43mm and travel 140mm. The shock is fully adjustable.

Thankfully Suzuki have upgraded the brakes. Brembo four-piston radial-mount calipers are featured and the bike now has ABS. Lighter and more rigid than conventional bolt-together calipers, the Hayabusas top-of-the-line radial-mount Brembo Monobloc front brake calipers deliver better feedback to the rider. The piston diameters were enlarged from 32-30mm to 32-32mm as larger pistons help apply greater force to the brake disc, which results in increased initial bite and a more controlled feeling.

A new standard equipment Antilock Brake System (ABS) unit features a lightweight, compact design. The ABS enhances brake performance by helping prevent, to a certain extent, wheel locking due to changes in road conditions or excessive braking, by matching stopping power to available traction.

THE HAYABUSA'S STYLING IS SO ICONIC THAT IT'S BEEN RETAINED TO THIS DAY...

the crankcase breather system.

Fuel injectors from the GSX-R1000 were also added, with 44mm throttle bodies and the Suzuki Dual Throttle Valve, with three selectable maps for different power delivery available.

The new exhaust was a heavier, four-into-two-into-one-into-two system.

Suspension was upgraded with 43mm Kayaba forks, including DLC coating, while a Kayaba rear shock was also aimed at providing a sportier ride.

The swingarm was strengthened, while a heavier-duty slipper clutch was added.

Tokico radial front brake calipers with smaller rotors also provided better performance with less weight, although more recently these have been swapped to Brembo items.

SPECIFICATIONS
SUZUKI GSX1300R HAYABUSA

CLAIMED POWER: 146kW[194hp]@9600rpm
CLAIMED TORQUE:
154Nm[114ft-lbs]@7200rpm
DRY WEIGHT: 220kg
FUEL CAPACITY: 21L

ENGINE: Liquid-cooled DOHC inline four-cylinder, 16-valve four stroke, TSCC, 81 x 65mm bore x stroke, 1340cc, 12.5:1 compression, Digital EMS with 32-bit, 1024kb ROM processor, 12-hole dual injectors per cylinder, 44mm throttle bodies, ram air, four-into-two-into-one-into-two stainless steel headers, cat converter, stainless steel tapered mufflers

GEARBOX: Six speed, constant mesh
CLUTCH: Wet multi-plate, hydraulic actuation, Final ratio: 18/43, Final drive: O-ring chain
CHASSIS: Twin spar alloy, steel sub-frame, Rake: 23.4°, Trail: 93mm

SUSPENSION: Fully adjustable 43mm KYB inverted forks, DLC (Diamond Like Coating), 120mm travel, fully adjustable KYB shock, 140mm travel

BRAKES: ABS, Dual 310mm rotors with four-piston radial-mount Brembo calipers, conventional master-cylinder, single 260mm rotor with single-piston Brembo caliper

WHEELS & TYRES: Cast alloy three-spoke, 3.50 x 17in, 6.00 x 17in, Bridgestone 120/70 – 17, 190/50 – 17

DIMENSIONS: Wheelbase: 1480mm, Ground clearance: 120mm, Seat height: 805mm, Overall height: 1165mm, Overall length: 2190mm, Overall width: 735mm

INSTRUMENTS: Analogue gauges and digital LCD info display

RIDE IMPRESSION

I dial up 3000rpm and the engine is just humming past idle, the ideal launch rpm for a Hayabusa. I pull in the clutch. Select first gear. Roll into stage and light the first staging light. I gently nudge the bike forward and light the second light up. A nice shallow stage. The clutch is deep in pull and I'm holding the bike back, my stomach hard into the tank, left leg on the 'peg ready to shift, right foot just touching the ground. Yellow. Yellow. Go!

I launch down Willowbank Drag Strip on the Hayabusa. The bike pulls hard in first, front wheel six inches off the deck. I grab second and the front touches down like a Boeing 747 then rapidly accelerates forward. Third. Fourth. Fifth gear. I cross the line with a 10.147@143.6mph. A 0.09 reaction time and a 1.8s 60ft have me smiling but it's not enough to be the fastest journo on the day – that went to Alex Gobert.

The acceleration and aerodynamics package of the Suzuki Hayabusa is that of legend. Until you run one down the chute and feel that top end, you just won't understand. Even hardened superbike racers get off these things grinning like crazy people. The faster you go, the faster the Hayabusa accelerates. A more addictive ride is yet to be produced by any manufacturer.

Suzuki Australia put on a great event for us all to sample the latest version of this iconic machine. The changes are new colours, Brembo calipers and a fantastic ABS system. Aside from that the bike is as per Gen2 original.

Heading off on the road ride I was instantly at home on the bike and within 10-minutes I was settled into what I call the 'Hayabusa Trance' where I seem to become more connected with the bike than usual – rolling into big fast turns and accelerating hard out of

them onto the next one.

A Hayabusa can be an extremely expressive and soul satisfying experience for any motorcyclist – I've spoken about this with other 'Busa riders and they too have found that place of 'Busa Zen – even the legend Shawn Giles knew what I was talking about when we chatted about the bike.

A combo of tighter, twistier corners came next and this is where the Hayabusa really surprises many newcomers – this bike may look bulky but under that aerodynamic bodywork is a nimble sports chassis that is amazingly capable in the tight stuff.

Throw in a few bumps and the solid nature of the bike and the extra weight makes for a stable ride that will leave many sportsbikes following its fat black lines on most roads.

On the open road the Hayabusa is

comfortable and vibration free. It pulls like a train from 3000rpm and is the ultimate mile-muncher. The gel seat is soft, footpegs rubber mounted (as is the top triple-clamp, thus the handlebars) and the screen, although low, offers great wind protection – as does the bodywork. Those with a regular pillion take note – there are few better two-up bikes on the planet...

While doing one of the photoshoot stops I had the opportunity to test the ABS brakes. Accelerating to 100km/h I simply jammed the lever on as hard as I could. The bike stopped in a perfect straight line, with the ABS intervening and preventing me from crashing (I was purposely trying to lock the front). I then followed with a more progressive emergency stop until the ABS again intervened, then finally an emergency stop just outside lock-up and the second brake test definitely got me stopped in a shorter distance.

Over the test loop, there was no brake fade, which was something that did present itself on the previous Tokico brake model. Feel and feedback is much, much better now. The brakes are sensational. **– JEFF WARE**

THE HAYABUSA PULLS LIKE A TRAIN FROM 3000RPM AND IS THE ULTIMATE MILE-MUNCHER...

ELECTRONICS

The fuel injection system was all new and was part of Suzuki's most powerful engine management system, controlled by a 32-bit, 1024kb ROM microprocessor.

The tapered 44mm throttle-bodies (up from 42mm) feature Suzuki's SDTV (Suzuki Dual Throttle Valve), with the primary butterfly's controlled by the throttle and the secondary butterflies controlled by the EMS.

Each throttle body has two 12-hole injectors. The primary injector is aimed at a steep 30-degree angle down the inlet port, to give optimum throttle response and operates at all times. The secondary injector is aimed at the secondary throttle valve and adds extra fuel at high rpm or high load conditions.

Primary injector on-time is controlled by the EMS via info from engine rpm, intake pressure and throttle position. On-time for the secondary injector is determined through rpm and throttle position. Another addition to the Hayabusa is the S-DMS (Suzuki Drive Mode Select) offering different maps for varying conditions.

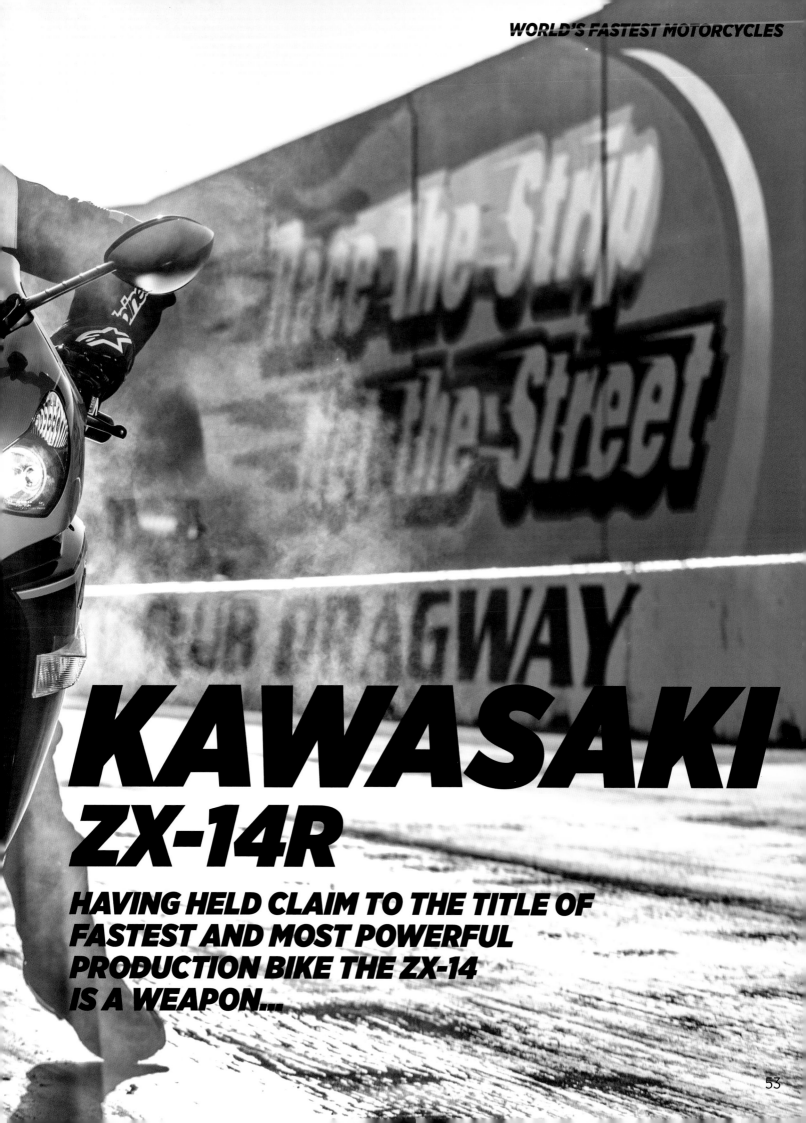

KAWASAKI
ZX-14R

HAVING HELD CLAIM TO THE TITLE OF FASTEST AND MOST POWERFUL PRODUCTION BIKE THE ZX-14 IS A WEAPON...

SPECIFICATIONS
KAWASAKI ZX-14R

COLOURS: Golden Blazed Green, Metallic Matte Carbon Grey

CLAIMED POWER: 147.2kW[197.1hp]@10,000rpm
CLAIMED TORQUE: 162.5Nm[119ft-lbs]@7500rpm
WEIGHT: 268kg
FUEL CAPACITY: 22L

ENGINE: Liquid-cooled, DOHC, inline four-cylinder four-stroke, 1441cc, 16-valve, 84mm x 65mm bore x stroke, 12.3:1 compression, Mikuni EFI 4 x 44mm throttle-bodies, KTRC traction control system

GEARBOX: Six-speed
CLUTCH: Wet, multiple-plate, hydraulic actuation
CHASSIS: Aluminium monocoque,
Rake: 23 degrees, Trail: 93mm

SUSPENSION: 43mm inverted fully adjustable forks, Uni-Trak monoshock, fully adjustable

BRAKES: ABS, 310mm semi-floating front petal rotors, radially mounted four-piston calipers, 250mm rear rotor, two-piston caliper

WHEELS & TYRES: 10-spoke, cast alloy, 1.75 x 17in, 120/70-17, 6.0 x 17in, 200/50-17

DIMENSIONS:
WHEELBASE: 1480mm,
SEAT HEIGHT: 800mm
OVERAL HEIGHT: 1170mm
OVERAL LENGTH: 2170mm

INSTRUMENTS: Analogue gauges and digital LCD info display

system providing 200hp from the 1352cc in-line four-cylinder when flat out, despite normally being limited to 190hp under normal riding conditions.

2006 would see the introduction of ABS as an option, while the 2007 model would come equipped with ABS and thanks to slight tweaks, boast an additional 3hp, both regularly and with the RAM Air system working.

In 2011 the press would see the new and improved ZX-14, a project led by Takeru Oshima and revealing a new larger capacity 1441cc engine – thanks to an additional 4mm of stroke, new more rigid frame and redesigned swingarm with an additional 10mm of length and more rigid design.

Additional engine changes include revised combustion chambers, and compression heightened to 12.3:1, while the port shapes have been revised, with larger exhaust pots as well. Styling was again revised, wheels were lighter items and an adjustable back-torque limiting clutch was added, along with a three-mode traction control system, to help keep all that power in check.

The Kawasaki ZX-14 was the bike to replace Kawasaki's ZX-12R, a bike which had been slated to take it to Suzuki's Hayabusa but which fell a little short of the mark when it came to reaching the highest speed possible.

This was partially attributed to the bike's aerodynamics which couldn't match those of the Hayabusa, despite having a slight edge with a claimed 178hp to the Suzuki's 175.

The reality was that the ZX-12R couldn't keep up in the race for top speed, with the ZX-14 released to make right this situation in 2005.

With vastly revised bodywork for greater aerodynamics the new ZX-14 was still electronically limited to 299km/h, thanks to an agreement between manufacturers but could post a staggering 0-60mph time of just 2.5 seconds.

At the time of release the ZX-14 was the fastest and most powerful production motorcycle ever built, with the RAM air

ENGINE

The engine has been taken from 1352cc to 1441cc through a 4mm increase in stroke to 65mm. The bore remains the same at 84mm. This has led to an increase in the mid-range and high rev horsepower, helped by a small reduction in the final drive ratio – the rear sprocket is up one tooth to 42. Kawasaki claims 147.2kW, boosted to 154.6kW by the Ram Air induction, although there's some caginess about this, with some staff suggesting the figures might prove to be even higher when magazines start to strap ZX-14s to dynos.

This is achieved by using revised combustion chamber shapes with a higher, 12.3:1 compression ratio and new intake and exhaust port shapes. These are hand finished, and the exhaust pots have a larger diameter to expedite gas flow from the engine. The exhaust headers are fatter for the same reason. The valve sizes are the same but the cam profiles feature increased lift. Internal pumping losses are reduced through increasing the size of bypass holes between the cylinders, and this is claimed to be a

major factor in the power increase.

Other changes are designed to maintain or improve durability, such as bigger small end bearings, a stronger crank and so on. But there's also a useful improvement in fuel consumption, made by automating the 'Economy' switch found on the 1400GTR. This advances the ignition timing significantly when engine loads are light (most of the time with a motor this powerful), and with other changes to the engine management has made the ZX-14 up to 20 per cent more fuel efficient, although most of the time an owner would expect to see an 8 per cent advantage over the outgoing model.

The additional power means additional heat to lose, so the radiator is fitted with a second fan while the bodywork more pronounced fins in the flanks of the fairing improve heat dissipation while keeping it away from the rider and passenger – Kawasaki says the amount reaching them is significantly reduced.

KAWASAKI CLAIMS 147.2KW, BOOSTED TO 154.6KW BY THE RAM AIR INDUCTION, ALTHOUGH THERE'S SOME CAGINESS ABOUT THIS...

Despite staggering power and torque on hand the ZX-14 remains agile and stable, with the electronics package helping provide confidence at the more extreme speeds available, although obviously there are few opportunities to put this to the test without a private test facility.

2014 also saw Kawasaki release the Special Edition Ohlins ZX-14R, which came with an Ohlins TTX39 rear shock, special paint and graphics, a seat cowl and gold wheels and rotor carriers. In 2015 this was again available but in a new Ebony and flame paint scheme, red calipers but standard black wheels.

DESPITE STAGGERING POWER THE ZX-14 REMAINS AGILE AND STABLE AT SPEED...

CHASSIS

The chassis is based on the old monocoque design and looks little different but has increased rigidity in the headstock and swingarm areas, while the swingarm itself is 10mm longer and more rigid. Stiffer springs are used in the suspension with revised damping to provide a sportier ride and sharper handling, aided by the fitment of lighter wheels –360g at the front and 1030g) at the rear. These wear versions of Bridgestone's new S20 Battlax rubber designed for heavyweight machines. The ABS system has been improved, particularly when braking on bumpy surfaces.

MINOR TWEAKS PROVIDE SPORTIER HANDLING...

ELECTRONICS & STYLING

The electronics keep pace with the latest from the European manufacturers, including Kawasaki's outstanding KTRC 3-mode predictive traction control system. Modes 1 and 2 are track-style options designed to maximise acceleration, as on the ZX-10R Ninja, while 3 is a safety mode for riding in poor conditions. They can be switched off altogether if required.

The system also differentiates between torque-induced wheelies, which it allows and more dangerous sudden ones, where it intervenes. In mode 3 all wheelies are prevented. There are two engine power modes, with Low Power reducing output from the midrange on by up to 25 per cent, and more usefully softening the throttle response across the range.

THE ZX-14 INCLUDES KAWASAKI'S OUTSTANDING KTRC 3-MODE PREDICTIVE TRACTION CONTROL SYSTEM

The styling meanwhile is recognisably ZX-14 but most noticeably with a more aggressive mien about the quad headlight visage. As mentioned, the side fines are more pronounced, and additionally the seat is new along with the tail section, although the same rear lights are used. The exhaust silencers are larger and a new shape.

The instruments now include ambient air temperature and, according to Kawasaki, a more accurate fuel gauge and range-to-empty reading. Everything is controlled via a switch on the left handlebar. The overall finish is very clean, with a lot of attention paid to keeping fasteners and brackets out of sight, while a pair of luggage hooks fold out neatly and with a satisfying click from beneath the seat.

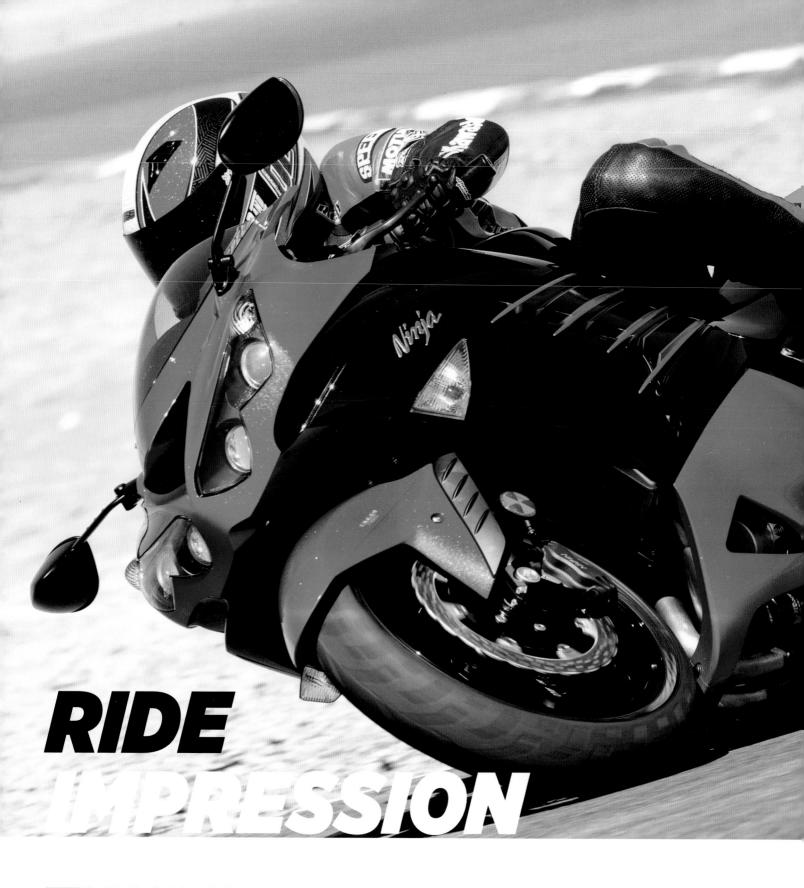

RIDE IMPRESSION

The ZX-14 is glitch-free off idle and from 5000rpm to the limiter there is some serious socket-popping torque on offer, with fantastic throttle response from anywhere above 7000rpm and wicked acceleration.

The ZX-14 we had on test made 182 rear wheel horsepower and a bucket load of torque. And it's the torque that really makes the difference. For example, our project GSX-R1000 was 172 rear wheel horsepower,

but I reckon, on a straight road, the 14 would beat the Gixer in fifth and sixth gears. It just keeps pulling and pulling and pulling like a steam train. At the drag strip I rode a stock engined, lowered Hayabusa back-to-back with the stock ZX-14 press bike and even after running a 10.5 on the 'Busa I was bored for the second-half of the chute. That's how fast the ZX-14 is up top!

On the open road the ZX-14 is smooth and comfortable but, for my 187cm, a little too

cramped. The footpegs are low and so is the seat, so there's not much room to move my long legs. I also copped bad wind blasting at freeway speeds as the wind hit me fair in the chest – thanks to the upright riding position, so if I owned a 14 I'd be throwing on a taller screen and adjustable rearsets. Holding rpm for constant speed is easy, but that flat spot is bang on 120km/h so a drop to fifth and even fourth is needed to pass on the freeway. Two-up the ZX-14 is great for both rider and pillion

as long as a bit more rear spring and comp is wound on.

The big, huge, grin-inducing surprise for me was the ZX-14s manners on the mountain. For a big chunk of motorcycle the 14 sure steers sweetly and requires much less forward planning and one-line commitment than a 'Busa or a Blackbird. Sure, for those of you used to cutting-edge sportsbike the 14 will feel like any big hyperbike, but to a hyperbike rider, the 14 will feel like a

sportsbike... The 23-degree steering angle and stiff monocoque frame work to make the ZX-14 steer quickly, precisely and with more confidence than its ZX-10R sibling on bumpy Aussie roads.

The 14 feels well balanced and settles and sits in a turn very, very well. Holding a line or changing line on demand – a trait not shared by the 'Busa or Blackbird – or the ZX-10R! With the rpm right the 14 fires off turns with ferocious speed but, with building momentum

behind you, pulling up the 14 for hairpins is a bit tough – but to be expected for a big bike and, again, better than its rivals. Still, a set of 320mm rotors would have been the go rather than the 310mm items lifted from the 10R...

Knee down scratching is a pleasure on this bike, and comes very naturally. The Bridgestones are fantastic on the 14 on the road and the only limitation to the bike is ground clearance. The fairing will scrap on the 14 – so having being pre-warned by a fellow

journo – I rode the bike around the problem, hanging off where possible. At least it kept the hoop on the fat part to cope with all the mumbo!

An extremely capable sportsbike that'd be awesome once set up...

The stock suspension settings on the 14 are a good all-round compromise but over choppy bumps I found the rear shock under sprung and over damped on compression. So a few clicks here and there and a bit more spring (I'm 98kg) did wonders. The forks were fine, if on the harsh side damping-wise for touring but if I were to own a 14 I'd leave them and just play with the clickers when required. I dialled in a bit more preload and comp as I was braking fairly hard on my local road, which has a lot of hairpins with bumps on entry...

The bike was rock solid otherwise, apart from the odd wallow through turns that you come to expect at almost triple the legal limit... The black lines are certainly fun though... **– JEFF WARE**

THE DESMOSEDICI IS A TRUE RACE REPLICA WITH NO COMPROMISES...

DUCATI
DESMOSEDICI RR

Announced at World Ducati Week in 2004, the Desmosedici RR would be revealed in 2006 at the Italian GP at Mugello, with just 1500 models to be produced over the models lifetime, while purchase priority was initially given to Ducati 999R owners.

When announced by Ducati in 2004, many

misconceptions surrounded the later 2006 unveiling, such as the fact that Ducati had decided to create the machine due to the move to 800cc MotoGP machines in the 2007 season – removing some of the need to protect the secrecy surrounding their bike. The truth seems to be however, that the Desmosedici RR was planned as far back as 2001, thanks to

Claudio Domenicali, Filipo Preziosi and Livio Suppo, with the race replica to be produced to assist in financing Ducati's racing.

Another fact that puts bunk to this suggestion is that although the Desmosedici RR shares many traits and similarities with the MotoGP machine, it isn't the same machine with road lights – with a number of different design choices made in order to ensure the bike would be suitable for road use.

Ducati did however make a huge effort to keep it as close to their racer as possible, a fact which no doubt caused issues during the production process, such as when they had to switch to a twin pulse firing order camshaft from the standard firing design they had originally developed.

When Ducati had originally joined MotoGP the first idea was to run a V-twin, more in keeping with the brand's road going creations, while also taking advantage of the regulations which limited the different engine configurations allowed to compete in various ways.

With well over the 200hp mark required for competitive racing in the MotoGP arena however, the level of performance and engineering that would be required to create a

ENGINE

True to its MotoGP derived origins, the Desmosedici was powered by an L-four cylinder, sharing the same bore and stroke of the GP machine, of 86 x 42.56mm, as well as the twin-pulse firing order, Desmodromic timing, titanium con-rods and IN and EX valves with chromium nitride coating, drilled and cut camshafts to reduce weight and pistons featuring double ribbed undercrown construction.

Both crankcases and the cylinder-head are sand-cast from aluminium, while the alternator casing and cam drive cover also sand-cast but in magnesium. The oil sump, clutch cover and cam covers are also magnesium, although pressure die-cast items.

The crankshaft is machined from a single forged steel piece, with a 70° crankpin offset that generates pulses at 0°, 90°, 290° and 380° for soft pulse timing, creating a smooth torque curve. The left and right pairs of pistons each share a crankpin, which combined with the 70° offset provides a compromise between regular even firing intervals and a Big Bang layout.

The race bike's dry sump was swapped for a more conventional wet-sump system due to the limited room available to fit an oil tank, while a number of features had to be added such as an alternator, battery, starter motor and all the associated additional wiring, while keeping the engine as compact and true to the GP machine as possible. With this in mind the engine was allowed to be 1cm wider on each side – the only compromise made.

Fueling is taken care of by Magneti Marelli fuel injection, featuring four 50mm throttle-bodies with 12-hole injectors, with the Desmosedici RR coming with a slip-on exhaust, as well as a full race-only exhaust with race-ECU to match. Volume on the race pipe is 102dB, with the quoted power figures taken with the race setup.

Power at the back wheel on the dyno was just under the 180hp figure.

A cassette-style gearbox is also used, staying true to the race machine, while a hydraulically actuated dry multi-plate slipper clutch is also used.

The exhaust system is a specifically developed four-into-two-into-one system with 42mm diameter tubing with a wall thickness of 0.8mm that exits through the tail via two vertical integrated exits.

THE DESMOSEDICI RR TOOK RACE REPLICAS TO A WHOLE NEW LEVEL IN THE SAME PERIOD CASEY STONER WOULD WIN DUCATI A WORLD CHAMPIONSHIP...

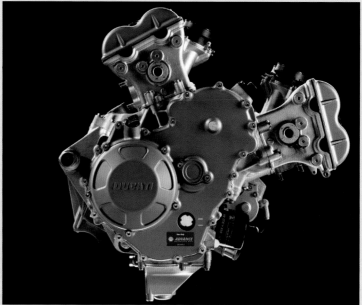

competitive V-twin meant that a V4 option was adopted instead, based upon the 90° L-twin engines previously developed.

What did make the Desmosedici RR so special was the fact that a manufacturer – particularly a smaller factory like Ducati – was producing the closest production bike you could buy to an actual GP bike – a claim that has throughout the ages been a massive selling point for passionate motorcyclists. Sales of the initial allocation of units, 500 in total are said to have been very fast – all spoken for within just five hours, while the increase in availability, eventually to 1500 saw less instantaneous success. This was blamed on a number of factors, although the fairest seems to be the steep asking price. This was also despite Casey Stoner winning Ducati's first MotoGP World

DUCATI MADE NO CONCESSIONS WITH THE DESMOSEDICI RR FOR A TRUE GLIMPSE INTO THEIR RACE MACHINES...

Championship in 2007.

Special inclusions such as a three-year warranty including free servicing, a race ECU with race-only exhaust system and full set of decals for the real race look only added to the exclusivity.

The bike itself featured a racing derived L-four 989cc engine, making use of the Desmodromic valve system and twin pulse firing order camshaft. Power was a claimed 200hp with the race exhaust and ECU fitted, while a dry weight figure of just 171kg made this a light machine with an impressive power to weight ratio. Brembo brakes with

Ohlins suspension promised high performance, while the traditional Ducati trellis frame was present, with MotoGP styled fairings, a single seat and exhaust through the tail.

The swingarm was a dual-sided unit, while Marchesini wheels were specially designed for this specific bike, with the same true for the Bridgestone tyres it would come fitted with.

Whether you're a Ducatisti or not, it's hard to argue with the impression made by the Desmosedici RR.

CHASSIS & BODYWORK

In the Desmosedici RR the engine is a stressed member, with the front steel trellis hybrid frame attaching to the front of the engine, while the swingarm pivots straight off the rear of the engine. The double-sided swingarm is fabricated from aluminium sheet, welded to a cast pivot section, while the wheelbase is a longer 1430mm to help keep the bike's power to the ground. Rake is also adjustable between 23.5° and 24.5°.

The rear subframe is a self-supporting carbon-fibre design, supporting the single rider seat.

Forks are 43mm USD FG353P Ohlins pressurised forks with TiN coated sliders, offering the first gas pressurised forks on a roadbike, with full adjustability, including compression damper adjusters, allowing balancing of the gas pressures between forks. The rear shock is also a Ohlins item, with rebound, high and low speed compression and preload adjustability.

Front brakes comprise massive semi-floating 330mm rotors,

graspsed by Brembo four-piston Monobloc calipers with 34mm pistons, while the rear features a 240mm rotor with twin-piston caliper, with 34mm pistons. The front lever is connected to a radial Brembo master-cylinder, with remote adjuster for on the move adjustment.

Wheels are also custom designed Marchesini forged magnesium alloy wheels, with a seven-spoke design to match the GP machines, while benefiting from a special protective coating to prevent stress corrosion failure. The wheels had to be beefed up to meet road requirements but are also machined to help reduce weight.

Tyres are special Bridgestone items, designed specifically for the Desmosedici RR.

All the bodywork of the Desmosedici RR is also carbon-fibre, including the fairings, mudguards, airbox, while the rear seat support is a high temperature resin carbon-fibre unit that

has to be able to withstand the exhaust temperatures pumped out with heavy use.

SPECIFICATIONS

DUCATI DESMOSEDICI RR

CLAIMED POWER: 147.1kW[200hp]@13800rpm
CLAIMED TORQUE: 116Nm[85.55ft-lbs]@10500rpm
DRY WEIGHT: 171kg
FUEL CAPACITY: 15L

ENGINE: Liquid-cooled DOHC L-four cylinder, 16-valve Desmodromic, gear-driven camshafts, 86 x 42.56mm bore x stroke, 989cc, 13.5:1 compression, four 50mm Magnetic Marelli throttlebodies, 12-hole microjet injectors, four-into-two-into-one vertical exit exhaust

GEARBOX: Six speed, cassette-type
CLUTCH: Dry multi-plate slipper clutch, hydraulically actuated
CHASSIS: Tubular steel trellis hybrid, aluminium swingarm, Rake: 23.5/24.5°, Trail: 98mm

SUSPENSION: Öhlins FG353P 43mm pressurised forks, preload, rebound and compression adjustment, TiN coated sliders, Öhlins rear shock, rebound, low/high speed compression, hydraulic preload adjustment

BRAKES: Dual 330mm semi-floating front rotors, radial Brembo Monobloc four-piston calipers, 240mm rear rotor, dual 34mm piston caliper

WHEELS & TYRES: Forged aluminium, 3.50 x 17in, 6.00 x 17in

DIMENSIONS:
WHEELBASE: 1430mm
GROUND CLEARANCE: N/A
SEAT HEIGHT: 830mm
OVERALL HEIGHT: N/A
OVERALL LENGTH: N/A
OVERALL WIDTH: N/A

INSTRUMENTS: Digital MotoGP derived unit

RIDE IMPRESSION

ON THE TRACK

Every now and then things happen that become a reference point in your life. It could be a disaster or the joy from the birth of your first child. These are the moments that categorise your life, and you will most definitely know when they occur.

I had one of these experiences with the Desmosedici RR. It was at Phillip Island where Ducati had granted selected journos access to the most exclusive and technically advanced motorcycle they'd ever created for sale to the public. I am talking, of course, about the D16RR, or Desmosedici RR.

This motorcycle exudes Ducati's wealth of racing experience. It is the best available, and represents a landmark in the history of motorcycling. Every component was selected for its performance benefit. Compromises were unacceptable. There had never been a machine this close to the equipment used to win GPs made available to regular people. Don't forget, Casey Stoner had just won the world championship on a machine only marginally different to the D16RR and here I was preparing to ride it!

I could feel my body shaking on the inside, like the first time I kissed a girl. It was extraordinary.

As we listened to a Ducati engineer's Desmosedici presentation, Craig McMartin flew past at speed, the tremendous note of the D16RR echoing through the pit garage, sending a shiver up my spine and leaving me tingling all over. Although it comes equipped with a street legal exhaust, the included race exhaust had been fitted to the test bike.

Now it was my time to ride the Desmosedici. That internal shake was now a visible one as I attempted to stay calm. It wasn't fear, just an intense excitement caused by the stream of adrenalin pulsing through my veins. The Italian technicians looking after the D16RR fitted fresh

"I'M SURE I SAW 300 ON THE SPEEDO, AND THE D16RR WAS STILL PULLING LIKE A BULLET TRAIN ON RED BULL..."

Bridgestones, and wheeled it out. I sat astride the exclusive kit and held the bars. My hands felt huge and the bike felt tiny, most likely a consequence of all the adrenalin.

Exiting pit lane, I gave it the berries into Doohan Corner and Southern Loop. I was acutely aware of the new tyres, and didn't want to throw $110,000 down the road, so I kept it very smooth and careful for the

first lap. The suspension was very rigid at lower speeds and the straight-line speed was awesome but what impressed me the most was the way it drove off turns. The traction available from the specially created Bridgestones was stupendous, aided no doubt by traction control.

Heading down Gardner Straight for the second time, I was going almost as fast as I dared when I selected top gear. The power

surge pushed me back into the rear of the seat. I'm sure I saw 300 on the speedo, and the D16RR was still pulling like a bullet train on Red Bull. My forehead started hurting due to the wind pressure on my helmet. At this speed the suspension was working properly and going into Doohan Corner, the D16RR felt as stable as Uluru.

Then, as I approached Lukey Heights, it happened. It was like I left my body and imagined I was Casey Stoner for the briefest of moments. I thought, "So this is what it feels like", at the very least it's as close as I will probably ever get. And it was sensational.

– Warwick Maguire.

MV AGUSTA
F4 312 RR

The MV Agusta F4 holds a special place in motorcycling history and is widely considered the reason that the iconic Italian brand is still in existence today.

Designed by Massimo Tamburini at the Cagiva Research Centre, who also worked on the Ducati 916, the F4 was created with the assistance of Ferrari and was based on a Ferrari Formula One engine from the early '90s, including the use of radial valves – a feature unique to the F4 at this time in production.

The first of the F4s was the F4 750 Serie Oro in 1999, with Oro meaning gold in Italian. 300 of this model were produced, with the swingarm, frame plates, and wheels all made from magnesium. All painted fairings and parts were carbon-fibre, including the fuel tank and airbox.

Also available at the same time was the F4 750 S, or Strada, which was a production version of the Oro, with aluminium replacing all the magnesium parts.

SPECIFICATIONS

MV AGUSTA F4 312 RR

CLAIMED POWER: 141.6kW[190hp]@12200rpm
CLAIMED TORQUE: 124Nm[91.5ft-lbs]@8200rpm
DRY WEIGHT: 192kg
FUEL CAPACITY: 21L

ENGINE: Liquid-cooled DOHC inline four-cylinder, 16-valve four stroke, 79 x 55mm, 1078cc, 13:1 compression, Weber-Marelli 5SM ignition, fuel-injection, four-into-two-into-one-into-two-into-four exhaust

Gearbox: Six speed, cassette type
CLUTCH: Wet multiplate, slipper
CHASSIS: CrMo steel tubular trellis, aluminium single-sided swingarm, Rake: 24.5°, Trail: 104mm

SUSPENSION: 50mm USD Marzocchi forks, 130mm travel, preload, compression and rebound damping adjustable, Sachs damper, 120mm wheel travel, preload, high- and low-speed compression and rebound damping adjustable

BRAKES: Dual 320mm front rotors, four-piston Brembo Monobloc calipers, 210mm rear rotor, four-piston caliper

WHEELS & TYRES: Marchesini forged aluminium, 3.50 x 17in, 6.00 x 17in, 120/70 x 17in, 190/50 x 17in

DIMENSIONS:
WHEELBASE: 1408mm
SEAT HEIGHT: 810mm

INSTRUMENTS: Digital dash, analogue tachometer

2001 would see a special Neiman Marcus Edition of the 750 S, with 10 available around the world.

In 2002 the F4 750 Senna was released, along with the Evo 02 model, with 300 Senna produced and sold to raise money for a charity founded by Ayrton Senna and had suspension

upgrades and limited carbon-fibre bodywork.

The final year of the F4 750 was in 2004 with the SPR and SR models, with the SPR featuring race livery, carbon-fibre parts and Marzzochi 50mm forks. The SR had the same engine with polished ports and high compression pistons but used Showa forks and

no carbon-fibre components.

2005 would see the introduction of the F4 1000, with the original AGO model featuring a number '1' inside a yellow circle on the fairings, with 300 produced.

The F4 1000 S was the regular model and included Marzocchi forks, Sachs shock and

ENGINE

MV's aim of giving the RR more low-down shove ensured that the first item on engineering chief Andrea Goggi's agenda was more cubes. Capacity is up from the F4 312's 998cc to match the 1078cc of the limited-edition F4 CC, via the bore being enlarged from 76 to 79mm. The cylinder head is modified to suit and also gets 10mm longer intake trumpets. Unlike Yamaha's rival R1 it doesn't get variable trumpets, which MV saves for limited edition models such as the F4 Tamburini and CC.

Even so, those changes – along with tweaked Marelli fuel-injection and smaller-section tailpipes for the high-level exhaust – are enough to increase maximum torque output from 115 to 124Nm, at 8200rpm instead of the previous 10,000rpm. Peak power output also goes up by 7bhp, from 183bhp at 12,400rpm to 190bhp produced 200rpm earlier. Other engine changes are taller first three ratios in the cassette gearbox and the addition of a slipper clutch.

MV'S AIM OF MORE LOW-DOWN SHOVE ENSURED THAT THE FIRST ITEM ON ENGINEERING CHIEF ANDREA GOGGI'S AGENDA WAS MORE CUBES...

CHASSIS

THE F4 312 RETAINS MV'S TUBULAR STEEL AND ALUMINIUM PLATE FRAME, WITH ITS SINGLE-SIDED SWINGARM...

The F4 312 retains MV's familiar tubular steel and aluminium plate frame, along with its aluminium single-sided swing-arm. Its main modifications are to the suspension, which is updated with damping internals at both ends. The 50mm Marzocchi upside-down forks also have carbon nitride coating plus fractionally more travel. The Sachs shock remains adjustable for both high- and low-speed compression damping, and can be adjusted for preload using an allen key.

Sachs also provides the adjustable transverse steering damper, as used by the F4 CC. Brembo supplies its top-of-the-range Monobloc radial calipers, along with a retained pair of 320mm front discs. And finally the RR 312 gets a smoked screen and revised headlight, both from the even more exotic F4 CC (the limited-edition special named after President Claudio Castiglioni), to complement its still gorgeous, Massimo Tamburini designed bodywork.

boasted 166hp. Also available was the F4 Tamburini, with the Torque Shift System for variable intake trumpets, while bodywork was all carbon-fibre.

The F4 1000 R was available in 2006, with Monobloc Brembo brakes, forged Brembo wheels, Marzocchi forks and did not include the Torque Shift System. The 1000 R set the fastest production class 1000cc motorcycle record in August of 2006.

A limited edition Senna model was also also available, with Brembo Goldline brakes, forked Marchesini wheels, 50mm Marzocchi forks and a lightweight Sachs shock. 300 were produced.

A F4 Veltro model was also available in the Strada – road, and Pista – race, with 99 Strada produced and 23 Pista.

The Veltros include the Torque Shift System, with the Strada featuring carbon-fibre bodywork and magnesium frame plates, with the Pista including a lightened frame, oversized radiator, carbon-fibre tank and magnesium triple-clamp and swingarm.

2006 also saw the F4 CC, named after Claudio Castiglioni – managing director of MV Agusta, with 200hp at the crank and a price tag of €100,000 (Euros), it featured a larger 1078cc engine, titanium valves, crank and piston rods, as well as the Torque Shift System.

2007 would see the first appearance of the F4 R 312, named after the bike's claimed top speed of 312km/h and boasting 183hp thanks to titanium intake valves, modified camshafts and 48mm throttle bodies.

From 2008 the F4 312 RR would use the 1078cc long-stroke version of the 312 engine, with torque available lower in the rev range as a result of the longer crankshaft. Adding the extra R, MV Agusta took a no compromise approach, with the RR featuring Monobloc Brembo calipers, 190hp and suspension calibration, revised exhaust pipes, a Sachs steering damper, clipper clutch, plus a new close ratio gearbox.

In 2015 the F4 RR represents the pinnacle of refinement, with Ride-by-Wire and four maps allowing total control over throttle sensitivity, torque, engine braking, engine response and the rev limiter. Inertial platform lean angle sensors and eight level traction control, with Ohlins electronic suspension, Brembo M50 Monobloc calipers, an electronically assisted quickshifter and Ohlins steering damper. Since 2014 however the bike returned to 998cc, from the larger 1078 engine featured in the 312 RR from 2008 through to 2013.

Only the F4 RC limited edition is more exclusive than the RR, with only 250 available.

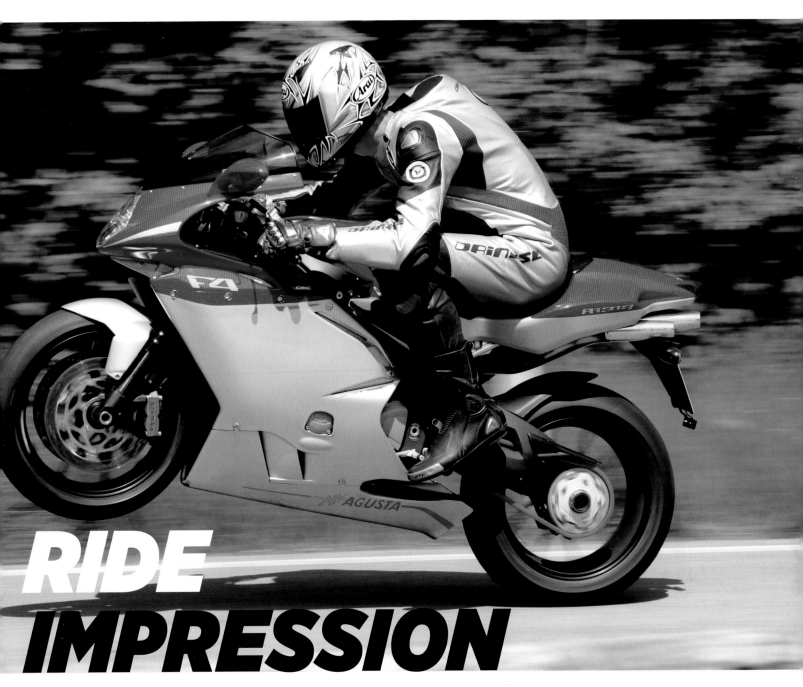

RIDE IMPRESSION

This fast and furious ride is the stuff that dreams are made of. I'm following an MV Agusta test pilot on a winding road near Varese, caning the Italian firm's exotic new F4 RR 312 on its home territory. The sun's shining, there's plenty of gas in the tank, and this latest RR is a more powerful still version of the radial-valve R 312 four that has been acclaimed as the world's fastest superbike.

My privileged position on the RR's thinly padded hot seat comes with one potential drawback – MV test riders are seriously quick, Marco is not hanging about on his favourite local roads – and failing to keep up would be embarrassing. But fortunately he's riding a naked Brutale while I'm on the super-sports F4 and equally importantly, this latest RR version of the F4 312 is proving as rider-friendly as it is rapid.

When Marco leaves his braking late for yet another blind bend, I can do likewise in the knowledge that the RR's Brembo Monoblocs will stop the bike on a five-cent piece, and that its supremely controlled yet improbably compliant suspension will make light of whatever surprises the turn holds. And when I find myself exiting a tightening bend a gear too high, I can rely on the MV to assist me with a flawlessly delivered and gloriously strong hit of torque from its ultra-flexible engine.

When Marco finally signals and pulls into a lay-by to compare notes and give his neck muscles a rest, I'm still right behind – and am seriously impressed not just by the sheer pace of the RR, but by how easy such a staggeringly quick bike has been to ride. MV's F4 has earned itself a fearsome reputation for both straight-line speed and racetrack performance

of late, especially since the R 312's launch. This version is not only faster still but also more sophisticated – almost polite.

Those attributes are less surprising when the RR's list of new features is examined, because MV clearly set out to add refinement as well as speed to the R 312. That bike earned its name with the top speed of 312km/h that it recorded at the Nardo speed-bowl in southern Italy. MV obtained that performance by tuning the previous F4 1000R with bigger titanium valves, hotter cams, larger throttle bodies and shorter intake trumpets – all mods designed to increase top-end power.

Despite the RR's ultra-racy initials, MV engine chief Andrea Goggi's aim when developing this year's follow-up was to boost performance lower down the rev range. That meant a 3mm bigger bore to increase capacity from 998

to 1078cc, along with mods to cylinder head, intake trumpets, fuel-injection and exhaust, and an uprated gearbox and clutch.

Along with boosting peak power output to 190bhp, that meant maximum torque not only going up by eight per cent, to 124Nm but being produced 1800rpm earlier, at just 8200rpm. The unchanged steel-and-aluminium frame holds revised Marzocchi forks and Sachs rear shock, plus Brembo's classy Monobloc radial calipers.

Bodywork is subtly revised with a headlight and smoked screen from the limited-edition F4 CC, and still seems stunningly sleek and fresh, despite minimal reworking since the original F4 750 was unveiled more than a decade ago.

The feeling of being aboard something truly special very much remains with this F4, too. That was emphasised when I pressed the starter button and the RR growled into life with a burble that turned into a series of racy yelps as the throttle was blipped. The bigger pistons certainly didn't prevent the radial-valve motor revving deliciously fast. But as I followed Marco out through the MV factory gates, along

the main road and up into the hills, the initial impression was one of restrained aggression and effortless control.

Inevitably, making a full evaluation of a 190bhp bike on these narrow roads was difficult-going-on-impossible, though at least the perfect weather was in marked contrast to the dampness of Monza on the R 312's track launch last year. Despite riding hard to keep up with the flying Marco I rarely saw more than 200km/h on the F4's digital speedometer – though the awesomely hard-accelerating RR doubtless hit higher figures on a few occasions when I didn't have time to glance down.

Whether the RR is good for even more than 312km/h remains to be seen although, as MV declines to follow the Japanese manufacturers by limiting its bikes' top speeds, there's no reason why this radial-valve rocket shouldn't be even faster than its predecessor.

What's for sure is that its midrange performance was stunningly strong, combining superbly precise throttle response with even more low-rev heft than I'd expected from its big-bore

powerplant, and seemingly with no more vibration than the familiar four-pot tingle at high revs.

I can also confirm that the RR's taller first few ratios, which would be useful on track, were no handicap on the road, as the motor had quite enough low-rev grunt for effortless pulling away. The way the MV stormed forward when I accelerated in first, picking up its front wheel in thrilling fashion even when I hauled my weight as far as possible over the front wheel, was truly mind-blowing.

The fact that the bike was honking through its airbox and howling through its shapely under-seat tailpipes made the experience even more addictive.

If the RR's flexibility and excellent fuelling were both very welcome at road-going speeds, the engine's other innovation, its slipper clutch, will be of more use on a racetrack. On these generally narrow and twisty roads I rarely needed to rev the 16-valve motor to its unchanged 13,000rpm limit, or to come crashing down through that sweet-shifting close-ratio box while braking hard into a bend, when the

mechanical slipper clutch would be most useful.

What my road ride did show was that the slipper clutch worked seamlessly in combination with MV's retained EBS (Engine Brake System), which delivers a small amount of fuel to one cylinder with the throttle closed. I didn't notice the RR's rear end feeling anything but stable and poised even when changing down while using the fearsomely powerful Monobloc calipers as hard as I dared, which suggests that the system did its job well. Those Monoblocs are another RR feature that will be most appreciated on the track, though contrary to some reports of other bikes I didn't find them over-sensitive for road use, at least in dry weather.

Although hard braking into turns occasionally generated a slight twitch from the front (doubtless curable with fine-tuning), the MV's other main chassis innovation, its revised and generally more compliant suspension, was generally welcome. With its decade-old basic engine and chassis layout the RR, which weighs 192kg dry (193kg for the 1+1 version), is far from the lightest super-sports four. But generally the

THE F4 IS WIDELY CONSIDERED THE REASON THAT THE ICONIC ITALIAN BRAND IS STILL IN EXISTENCE...

MV hid its weight very well. Its unchanged and finely honed geometry allowed it to be flicked into bends with speed and confidence.

A defining moment for the chassis came when I pitched the F4 into a fast, right-hander that was shaded from the bright sunlight by overhanging trees – and realised, when fully committed, that the surface under those trees was actually horribly pitted. Some bikes, even good bikes, would have struggled, but the RR didn't even twitch. Its suspension absorbed the bumps, its Dunlop Sportmax Qualifiers stuck hard, and the bike swept through the bend as though it was lapping smooth-surfaced Monza, its spiritual home.

The perfect end to my test would have been to blast down the A8 autostrada to nearby Monza (well not that nearby, but the 70km wouldn't have taken long at 300km/h-plus) to put the

RR through its paces at the track where both its immediate predecessor and the original F4 750 Serie Oro were launched. Instead I found myself back on the main road to Varese, being held up by smelly trucks and Alfa saloons through the traffic while trying not to get too annoyed at this waste of the RR's high-speed potential.

Exactly, in other words, as the RR will be ridden by most of its owners for much of the time. And once again, on these too-busy roads it was the MV's midrange grunt, precise fuelling and relatively compliant suspension that made the ride fun – at least in short bursts – rather than merely painful and frustrating. Confirming that the F4 RR 312 is not only almost certainly the fastest mass-produced streetbike that MV Agusta has ever built, it's also surely the best yet.

– ROLAND BROWN

YAMAHA V-MAX

THE FASTEST ACCELERATING YAMAHA STREET BIKE EVER BUILT...

Yamaha's V-Max was originally released in 1985 and forged itself a reputation for insane performance, with the 1985 model in production until 2007 with only minor updates during this period.

The design team for the V-Max was led by Akira Araki, with much of the design credited to Atsushi Ichijo, with additional input from Ed Burke and John Reed.

In 1993 the main update to the V-Max included larger forks, four-piston calipers and other updates to help handling and safety, with the bike's cornering and suspension, but not power, an area of common criticism.

ENGINE

Powering the VMAX is a 1679cc liquid-cooled four-stroke DOHC 65 degree V4 engine. Running with bore x stroke dimensions of 90.0 x 66.0mm (compared to 76.0 x 66.0mm for the old V-MAX) and featuring a compression ratio of 11.3:1, the powerplant develops 147.2kW or 197hp at 9000rpm, together with a huge torque output of 166.8Nm or 123ft-lbs at 6500rpm.

The VMAX benefits from advanced Yamaha G.E.N.I.C.H (Genesis in Electronic engineering aimed at Innovative Control technology based on Human sensibilities) technology with features such as YCC-I (Yamaha Chip Controlled Intake) and YCC-T (Yamaha Chip Controlled Throttle) which are key factors in achieving the engine's high levels of power. This high-tech engine is the first Yamaha V4 to be equipped with a sophisticated fuel injection system.

In order to achieve a rapid and efficient combustion process Yamaha engineers have designed a four-valve pent-roof combustion chamber. For such a large capacity engine with its massive bores, these high-efficiency combustion chambers are remarkably compact, and their space-saving design has been facilitated by the introduction of an ingenious camshaft drive system.

On a conventional DOHC engine, the intake and exhaust camshafts are usually driven by one chain, but Yamaha engineers have designed a system which the intake camshaft is driven by a chain, while the exhaust camshaft is driven by a gear mechanism. This innovative combined chain and gear cam drive minimizes the pitch between the intake and

BOASTING 200HP THE VMAX IS ONE OF THE MOST EXTREME MUSCLE BIKES AVAILABLE, WITH A STAGGERING 166NM OF TORQUE ON TAP...

exhaust camshafts, which in turn permits a much more compact cylinder head design. The VMAX also runs with Iridium spark plugs.

The use of the space-saving combined cam drive has allowed a narrower valve angle of 14° IN and 15° EX, giving a total of 29°. This narrow valve angle helps to minimize engine dimensions, while also permitting the use of optimised port shapes.

Yamaha engineers have also reduced the overall weight of the valve train assembly by using an inner shim type valve clearance adjustment system, as opposed to the outer shim system on the previous VMAX engine.

Despite the fact that engine features a 40 per cent increase in cubic capacity compared to the old model, the V4 powerplant's overall dimensions are remarkably compact.

In order to keep the engine's front-to-rear length as short as possible, it adopts a 65°

V-bank, compared to 70° on the original VMAX. This narrower angle between the massive cylinders serves to concentrate mass for more neutral handling performance, and makes the powerplant 27mm shorter than the original.

Also, the use of a centrally located cam chain helps to minimize the engine's width. Despite the fact that the bore dimensions on the larger-capacity VMAX are over 18 per cent larger than its predecessor, the engine's overall width is about the same as the older model, and overall height is only 6.5mm taller.

Another example of the way in which sophisticated technology has been used to enhance the performance on the VMAX is evident in the forged aluminium pistons.

Fracture-split (FS) carburised conrods were first used on the 2004 model YZF-R1, and in order to handle the huge power and torque output of the 1679cc V4 engine, this

technology is now featured on the VMAX.

The YCC-I (Yamaha Chip Controlled Intake) system is designed to vary the intake funnel length so that it is 'tuned' to give a positive intake pulse that best suits the prevailing engine speed.

When engine revs rise above 6650rpm, electronically-controlled servomotors cause each intake funnel to separate instantaneously, effectively creating a shorter intake funnel measuring only 54mm from 150mm, which enables the VMAX engine to deliver even stronger performance from the mid-range right through to peak rpm.

Another highly advanced feature seen on the VMAX is the YCC-T throttle, which features the same design as that used on the Yamaha supersport models.

This innovative throttle has a remarkably high calculating speed, and assesses the engine's running conditions every millisecond, which enables the system to respond instantaneously to rider inputs.

Aggressively-styled hand-finished aluminium air intakes mounted on the front left and front right side of the dummy fuel tank give the VMAX a muscular profile, and direct an intense flow of air straight into the massive airbox which is approximately twice the volume of the design on the original model.

To complement the machine's more powerful 1679cc V4 engine, a compact shaft drive system has been designed for the VMAX. By optimising the ratios of the engine-side reduction gear and the final gear, engineers have designed a smaller-diameter rear gear case. Featuring 29 teeth compared to 33 on the older model, the slimmer and more compact case measures 188mm.

An 02 sensor (Lambda sensor) detects oxygen levels in the stainless-steel/titanium exhaust system and regulates the fuel supply via the fuel injection system to ensure that emissions are minimised, while a three-way honeycomb catalyser ensures the VMAX exceeds EU3 regulations.

For reduced weight and a high quality finish, the clutch cover, AC magneto cover and drive shaft cover are all manufactured from lightweight magnesium alloy.

A sophisticated cooling system, which consists of two radiators and an oil cooler keep the temp under control. The two-piece radiator features a curved-type upper section, which allows the engine to be situated closer to the front wheel for idealised mass centralisation. In order to achieve a maximum surface area for highly efficient engine cooling, the lower part of this two-piece radiator is a conventional flat shape whose unobtrusive design allows the massive V4 engine to be seen in all its glory – and at the same time permits the fitment of a fan.

And to ensure stable oil temperatures for consistently strong engine performance, the 1679cc engine is equipped with a liquid-type oil cooler.

The V-Max originally used a tuned version of the V4 engine from the Yamaha Venture, with the addition of the V-Boost system, which controls butterfly valves in the intake manifolds between pairs of cylinders.

The valves are opened starting at 5750rpm and are fully open by 8000rpm, with a claimed 10 per cent increase in power on the top end.

The current generation of Yamaha's V-Max, or VMAX as it is now called first appeared in 2008 and became available in 2009 and was a massively overhauled version of the original, still featuring a DOHC V4 engine but with a capacity of 1679cc compared to the original's 1197cc.

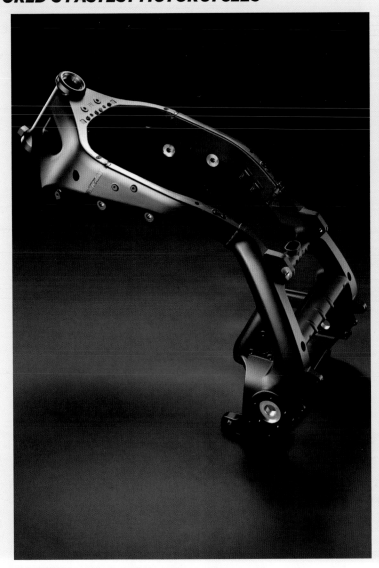

CHASSIS

The VMAX's diamond-type frame has been developed using Yamaha's industry-leading chassis design and manufacturing technology, and features an immensely strong yet lightweight structure that is made up from a variety of gravity-cast, CF die-cast and extruded aluminium sections.

This innovative design incorporates gravity-cast components for the main frame and pivot assembly, while the rear frame is made from a range of exclusive CF die-cast and extruded parts, which are welded together. This combination of these different types of aluminium, each with a different rigidity level, is one of the major factors in achieving the desired balance of rigidity.

To fine-tune this balance even further for excellent handling and accurate rider feedback, the wall thickness on the main frame varies from between 3mm through to 6mm.

An imaginary straight line drawn between the pivot and head pipe runs right through the centre of the V-bank and this layout makes for neutral handling characteristics. And by incorporating the V4 engine as a stressed member – using cast-iron mounts at the front, the centre of the V bank and at the top and bottom of the crankcase – the overall chassis rigidity balance is further enhanced.

The bike's swingarm is over 35 per cent longer than on the existing model at 662.5mm, allowing the rider to lay down the 1679cc V4 engine's power more effectively than ever.

The 52mm fork tubes offer excellent rigidity combined with smooth fork action – and they benefit from an oxidized titanium coating that ensures increased surface hardness and stiction-free operation – while the dark finish perfectly complements the black frame and engine.

The front suspension is designed to deliver a smooth ride with neutral handling and is fully adjustable for preload as well as rebound and compression damping.

It's not only the massive 52mm tubes that put these forks in a league of their own – they also feature two-piece outer tubes. Featuring an extremely rigid cast lower section incorporating the radial-mounted brake calipers and an extruded aluminium upper section that has been precision-machined for superior suspension action, these special front forks characterise the VMAX's inherent style, first-class quality and advanced technology.

The combination of flex-resistant 52mm tubes, a cast aluminium upper triple-clamp and forged aluminium lower triple-clamp, as well as a wide pitch of 225mm and 30mm offset ensures neutral steering.

The rear suspension is a link-type Monocross system that is also adjustable for preload, as well as for compression and rebound damping.

For added convenience, the VMAX is equipped with a hydraulic remote adjuster for preload setting, while a remote control

dial beneath the tandem footrest adjusts the compression damping. Another remote control dial beneath the left-side swingarm allows easy adjustment of the rear shock's rebound damping.

The braking system that has been developed for the VMAX is one of the most sophisticated and powerful designs ever seen on a Yamaha motorcycle. At the front end, dual 320mm diameter wave-type rotors are gripped by radial-mount six-piston calipers and a Brembo radial-pull master-cylinder.

A 298mm wave-type rotor on the rear is slowed by a pin-slide type single-piston caliper. The VMAX is also equipped with a specially developed linear-controlled hydraulic ABS system that is designed to enhance braking control over a variety of road surfaces and in varying riding conditions.

This innovative and compact ABS system combines the ECU and hydraulic mechanism into a single unit that is situated under the seat. By keeping the system's dimensions to a minimum, neither the machine's aesthetics or weight have been compromised and the positioning of the unit ensures that overall mass centralisation is enhanced.

For natural handling qualities the VMAX is equipped with 18-inch front and rear wheels that are shod with specially developed BT028 tyres that are designed to offer the optimum balance of grip, shock absorption and roadholding.

AN ALL NEW CHASSIS, LENGTHENED SWINGARM AND GREATLY UPRATED SUSPENSION ON THE NEW VMAX PUT TO REST EARLIER MODEL HANDLING COMPLAINTS...

SPECIFICATIONS
Yamaha VMAX

CLAIMED POWER:
147.2kW[197hp]@9000rpm
CLAIMED TORQUE:
166.8Nm[123ft-lbs]@6500rpm
WET WEIGHT:
310kg (full tank, oil and coolant)
FUEL CAPACITY: 15L

ENGINE: G.E.N.I.C.H, liquid-cooled, DOHC, four-valve, 65-degree V4, four-stroke, 90 x 66mm bore x stroke, 1679cc, 11.3:1 compression, YCC-I intake, YCC-T throttle, quad 48mm throttle-bodies, quad 12-hole injectors, titanium/stainless steel four-into-one-into-two-into-four, shaft final drive

GEARBOX: Five-speed constant mesh
CLUTCH: Wet multi-plate 19-plate slipper clutch, diaphragm spring
CHASSIS: Aluminium cast and extruded diamond-shaped Delta Box, Rake: 31°, Trail: 148mm

SUSPENSION: 52mm oxidised titanium coated conventional forks, fully adjustable, 120mm travel, Monocross link-type fully adjustable (all remote) shock, 110mm travel

BRAKES: ABS, Dual 320mm floating front wave rotors, six-piston radial-mount calipers, Brembo radial-pull master-cylinder, single 298mm floating rear wave rotor, pin-slide single-piston caliper

WHEELS & TYRES: Cast alloy five spoke, 3.50 x 18in, 6.00 x 18in, Bridgestone BT028 120/70 – 18, 200/50 – 18

DIMENSIONS: Seat height: 775mm, Overall height: 1190mm, Overall length: 2395mm, Wheelbase: 1700mm

INSTRUMENTS: Electronic fuel tank mounted display with temp, trips, live fuel, throttle angle opening, stop watch and count down, intake temp, gear position – dash display with digital speed, analogue tacho, programmable shift light

Power was up to 174hp (claimed) compared to the original's more tame 113hp, which while impressive in 1985 was just the norm towards the last few years of production. Torque was likewise massively boosted to 113ft-lbs, an increase in 30ft-lbs, with fuel injection replacing the original carbs.

The original V-Boost system was also replaced by Yamaha Chip Controlled Intake (YCC-I), with the intake system shortened at higher rpm by a servo which lifts the airhorns – a concept invented by Massimo Tamburini. Meanwhile the Yamaha Chip Controlled Throttle (YCC-T) uses a G.E.N.I.C.H. computer to compute the best throttle position, ignition advance, EXUP valve position and injection time.

Other additions to the new model included a slipper clutch, ABS with six-piston calipers on the front end, fully adjustable suspension and a cast aluminium frame.

Wet weight was also up to 315kg, with the 15L tank purported to not offer the largest range, particularly if the bike was being ridden aggressively.

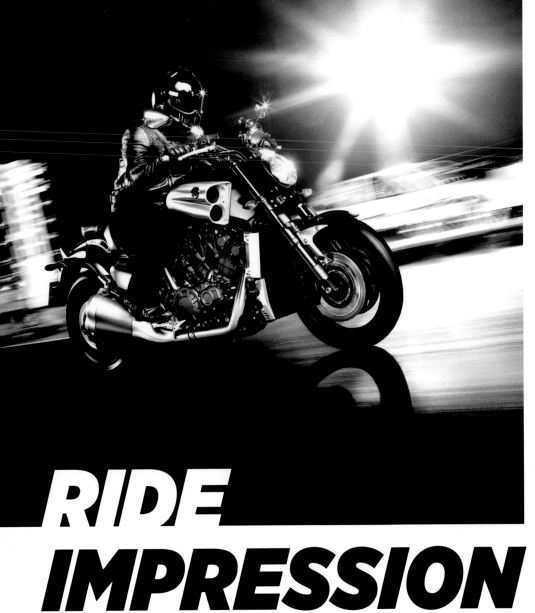

RIDE IMPRESSION

Cutting straight to the point, I'm going to answer the question on the tip of everyone's tonque.

Yes. The VMAX is quicker than a Hayabusa, ZX-14, B-King, K 1200 S and everything else on the street. Make no mistake. This is no H-D wannabe cruiser. This is a wild machine that'll knock your boots off and strain your neck. This is the ultimate in acceleration-induced adrenaline. And stupid fun. Really stupid fun!

Throwing a leg over the VMAX for the first time reveals the hefty weight of the machine. Although COG is kept low and forward, there's no way to hide 310-kilograms (wet), however a low seat helps.

The 'bars are fantastic – solid tapered alloy items at a comfy height. Controls are light and fall to hand well and although a bit high the 'pegs are well placed for me at 185cm. My only initial gripe is that my knees well and truly sit either-side of the big air intakes, about 150mm above the knee cut-outs in the frame rail/seat upper area. Built for those of shorter status I suspect!

As we fire the bikes into life and gear up, the air is filled with anticipation. A dozen or so Russian, Japanese, Canadian and UK journos – along with us Aussies – all eager to ride flat stick ASAP!

We follow a lead rider on our day-long loop, which takes us through some of the best twisties I've ever encountered, plus some big straights and back through the city to the beach area...

Rolling out of the Ranch the bike feels cumbersome and like any heavily raked bike below 40km/h it wants to drop the steering either side, so takes some time to get used to.

Within a few minutes I can't help but drop back 200-metres from the group and nail the throttle. What happens next is not what I expect. The VMAX throttle response is instant. And I mean instant like I've never felt before from a production machine.

The millisecond I snap the throttle open the VMAX slams my butt into the seat hump and hauls forward with huge pace. From 4000rpm the bike starts to pull hard but once the tacho swings past 6500rpm the rest of the ride is a blur. Not only that. The fat rear hoop lights up and gently drifts left as the bike takes me along for the ride. Fun factor? 10 out of 10!

I notice the rest of the pack doing similar things. Dropping back in my mirror, then closing up on me with rapid pace. There must be lots of grinning going on...

By the time we reach our first stop for tracking

photos there's grin all around and lots of "Man, how quick is this thing?" comments flying. The Japanese boss looks happy. And deservedly so. No engine has impressed the world motorcycle press this much since the GSX-R1000 was born... But that donk doesn't even come close...

With police closing the road just so we can do tracking shots, I have the opportunity to stretch the VMAX V4's 'rods to the limit. On return from my photo session to the next one up the hill and with the knowledge that there was no traffic ahead, I nail the bike. First gear to the limiter is breathtaking. Second to the limiter and still pulling like first. Third and only now the rear hoops starts to hook up properly and even so, the acceleration is so intense that my glasses are up on my forehead and my chinstrap is choking me!

I grab fourth gear and nail it. Bloody hell! The same pull as first gear. This is insane. Fifth is no different. I roll off to prepare for a corner and after washing off speed the dash still shows 210km/h. I didn't get a top speed but it was well over the limited 220km/h. If the bike is rolled on the limiter works but I assume it is bypassed if the bike is nailed from a standstill. Either that or the limiter is disarmed on the press bikes...

Each gearshift is precise and the close-ratio (in sports cruiser terms) with a tall top gear 'box is well matched to the smooth engine power delivery. Monster torque starts from as low as 1500rpm and instant acceleration is on tap anywhere, however, from 6500rpm to the limiter the V4 is nuts. Particularly around 7000rpm where all of the planets align and the rocket ship heads to space. It really is an addictive feeling...

OK, so this is no cornering sportsbike. Yes, it understeers off turns when pushed. Yes, it has limited ground clearance and of course it suffers from bump steer. But compare it to any other sports cruiser on the market and the VMAX handles like a sportsbike. The brakes are sensational. And as we head up and over the hills through Pallamar State Mountain Reserve I discover what a capable machine the VMAX is. Riding at a fast pace is possible with smooth inputs and respect for the bike's not unsubstantial weight. The braking package is sensational and on par with any sportsbike, with only some fade after a good 35-kilometres of downhill twisties. The 'pegs touch down smoothly and the bike is composed throughout cornering, only being upset

> **"THE ACCELERATION IS SO INTENSE THAT MY GLASSES ARE UP ON MY FOREHEAD AND MY CHINSTRAP IS CHOKING ME!"**

STYLING

Mass centralisation was one of the key goals for the VMAX development team. During the machine's exhaustive development and testing phase, every effort was made to use lightweight materials wherever possible – and at the same time, to locate heavier components close to the bike's centre of mass.

One of the most significant factors in achieving an idealised mass centralisation is the positioning of the 15-litre fuel tank under the seat. Manufactured from light fluorinated polyethylene, the tank is easily accessed by means of a lever with a built-in damper.

Mounted on top of the dummy fuel tank is a multi-function Organic Electro-Luminescent OEL instrument panel that displays a wide range of information on its 256x64 dot display. This ly designed OEL panel gives a bright, easy-to-read display and offers an instant response and its functions include odometer, tripmeter, clock, fuel gauge, temperature gauge, gear position, running fuel consumption, intake air temperature and throttle opening, as well as a stopwatch with a countdown function.

The fact that the styling on the original VMAX has remained largely unchanged for 24-years is a tribute to the immense strength and unique character of its original design. Creating a worthy successor to this iconic motorcycle posed many challenges for Yamaha's team of designers.

While the original VMAX embodied the spirit of the drag strip the model has been designed to radiate a feeling of massive internal strength that hints at the awesome power just waiting to be unleashed at any time. Key to this imagery are the four massive air intakes, the muscular V4 engine, and the four short upswept mufflers.

by bumps mid-turn. Rear rebound is a little quick but the remote adjusters make life very easy.

The Bridgestone tyres offer good grip, traction and fair feedback considering the machine's size. Front feel is a little lacking but not a problem. If you want to go knee scraping, buy an R1... That said, cornering can be enjoyed all day on the VMAX.

As the road opens up I start to have a bit of fun with the throttle, laying some big fat third gear blackies for Toshi Arakaki, the ex-500 GP rider and current All Japan racer and journo, who was riding with me. He returns the favour with some of the most smokin' sideways drifts you can imagine.

You don't need to be an ex-500 GP rider to smoke up the VMAX though – as it'll do it in the first three gears easily. A great way to impress your mates that's for sure!

Yep. There wasn't much stone left in that rear Bridgestone at the end of the day, that's for sure...
– JEFF WARE

APRILIA RSV4

APRILIA'S SUPERBIKE BREAKS THE 200HP BARRIER...

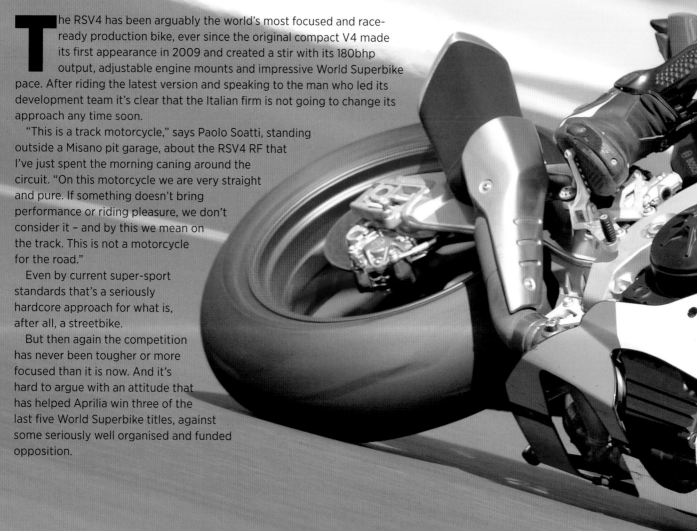

The RSV4 has been arguably the world's most focused and race-ready production bike, ever since the original compact V4 made its first appearance in 2009 and created a stir with its 180bhp output, adjustable engine mounts and impressive World Superbike pace. After riding the latest version and speaking to the man who led its development team it's clear that the Italian firm is not going to change its approach any time soon.

"This is a track motorcycle," says Paolo Soatti, standing outside a Misano pit garage, about the RSV4 RF that I've just spent the morning caning around the circuit. "On this motorcycle we are very straight and pure. If something doesn't bring performance or riding pleasure, we don't consider it – and by this we mean on the track. This is not a motorcycle for the road."

Even by current super-sport standards that's a seriously hardcore approach for what is, after all, a streetbike.

But then again the competition has never been tougher or more focused than it is now. And it's hard to argue with an attitude that has helped Aprilia win three of the last five World Superbike titles, against some seriously well organised and funded opposition.

That focus has also brought the RSV4 victories in countless comparison tests, even if the resultant sales haven't come close to matching that level of success. So it's perhaps not surprising that, when revamping the RSV4, Aprilia have remained true to their no-compromise path and continued to tune and tweak the compact V4 to shave even more tenths of a second off its lap times.

That means you'll find more horsepower, less weight and more refined electronics on the latest base model RSV4 RR and you'll find all that plus Öhlins suspension and forged wheels as part of the package on the higher-spec RSV4 RF – the equivalent of Aprilia's old Factory designation – that is the only model being imported to some markets.

But don't bother looking for rider-friendly features like the rival BMW S 1000 RR's heated grips and cruise control, or even a semi-active

suspension option, on this pure-bred Italian.

Increased power was a major consideration, as it had to be with the super-sports bar now raised to a 200bhp level that would have been unthinkable just a few years ago.

The 65-degree V4 unit remains 999cc but is extensively modified, with numerous lightened internals including the conrods and reaches the double-ton with a claimed maximum output of 201bhp at 13,000rpm.

The RSV4 design has always benefitted from the closeness of Aprilia's road and racing divisions, and that is perhaps more true than ever. The firm's race operation is now headed by Romano Albesiano, who was in charge of the RSV4 project from its beginning, so it's no surprise that much of the latest model's technology comes straight from the track.

"Romano Albesiano was the father of this motorcycle, so when we started this project he

really wanted to make a contribution to it, says Soatti. "At one stage we were in a bit of a cul-de-sac with the inlet funnels, because we had many, many solutions but none was working really well. So we went to Romano and said, 'You have to give us this team of yours that has a lot of experience of funnels.' They have a database of information, and within a matter of weeks we found a really good solution."

Chassis changes are less extensive, and are mainly aimed at maintaining stability with the increased power. The engine is lowered in the frame, steering geometry is quickened via reduced trail, and the swing-arm is lengthened. Aprilia's high-tech APRC electronics package is updated with Bosch's lean-angle sensor, and the Brembo Monobloc brake calipers gain a higher specification Race ABS system. Weight is down by a few kilos, to just 190kg without fuel.

ENGINE

As always the RSV4's heart is an ultra-compact, 65° V4 with DOHC valve operation and 16-valves. The engine's dimensions of 78 x 52.3mm are unchanged since the original model. So too is the camshaft drive arrangement, by lateral chain to the intake cam, then gear to the exhaust cam, allowing very compact cylinder heads.

The current generation gets a revised airbox and variable-length intake trumpets, larger inlet valves, and exhaust valves that follow the inlets by also now being made from titanium. Forged camshafts are lighter, as are the new Pankl conrods, smaller crank pins and the transmission system's narrower gears.

The engine also has CNC-machined combustion chambers that allow tighter tolerances, a redesigned sump and crankcases to reduce friction from its oil, and a exhaust system with larger, 36mm (from 33mm) diameter downpipes that are squeezed into the same space in the ultra-compact bike.

The experience of Aprilia's race department was important in shaping the exhaust and also in fine-tuning the design of the variable length inlet trumpets, whose design benefits from the firm's World Superbike experience.

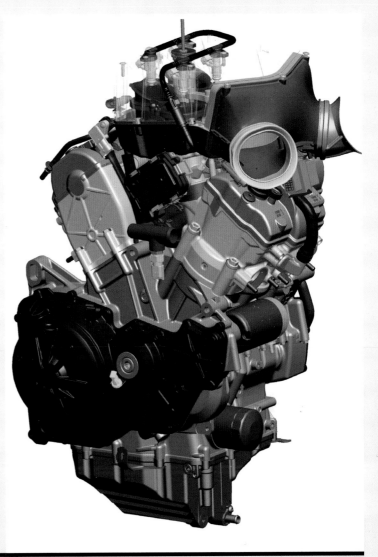

AS ALWAYS THE RSV4'S HEART IS AN ULTRA-COMPACT 65° V4...

CHASSIS

THE ORIGINAL RSV4 WAS UNIQUE IN HAVING ADJUSTABLE ENGINE MOUNTS...

The original RSV4 was unique in having adjustable engine mounts built into its compact twin-spar aluminium frame, initially to benefit World Superbike racers.

This is now used to lower the centre of gravity slightly by bolting the V4 unit in its lowest position. The swing-arm is lengthened by 4mm (with potential for an additional 9mm), and the steering geometry is quickened by slightly reduced trail. Overall weight is down by a few kilos, to just 180kg without fuel.

The base-model RSV4 RR has Sachs suspension and steering damper and is upgraded to include some features from the old Factory model, such as magnesium sump and cylinder head covers and variable-length intake ducts.

The RSV4 RF, produced in a limited edition of 500 units with red/white/black "Superpole" paint scheme, includes the RR's optional Race Pack of forged wheels plus Öhlins suspension and steering damper.

STYLING & ELECTRONICS

The RSV4 comes in two versions, of which only the higher spec RF model is available in some markets.

Advanced electronics have been one of the RSV4's main assets since the APRC (Aprilia Performance Ride Control) model of 2011 and the system is updated to include Bosch's latest lean-angle sensor. The traction control and anti-wheelie control are recalibrated, you still get launch control and a quick-shifter and the brake system now also includes a Race ABS system with its Brembo Monobloc calipers.

Both models can also be fitted with the accessory V4-MP software, the MP standing for Multimedia Platform, basically a GPS-enabled telemetry system that connects the bike to a smartphone.

This allows downloading of data after riding, plus the ability to fine-tune traction control and anti-wheelie for individual corners, provided the track in question is on Aprilia's list of major circuits.

SPECIFICATIONS
APRILIA RSV4 RF (RR)

CLAIMED POWER:
150kW[201bhp]@13000rpm
CLAIMED TORQUE:
115Nm[85ft-lbs]@10500rpm
DRY WEIGHT: 180kg
FUEL CAPACITY: 18.5L

ENGINE: Liquid-cooled, DOHC 65° V4, 16-valve four stroke, 78 x 52.3mm bore x stroke, 999cc, 13.6:1 compression, four Marelli injectors, four Dell'Orto 48mm throttle bodies, ATC, RbW, ABS, AQS, AWC, ALC, four-into-two-into-one silencer,

GEARBOX: Six speed, cassette-type
CLUTCH: Wet multi-plate, mechanical slipper system
CHASSIS: Aluminium perimeter frame, adjustable headstock, rake engine height, swingarm pivot height, double-braced aluminium swingarm, Rake: 26.5°, Trail: 104mm

SUSPENSION: Fully adjustable 43mm Ohlins inverted forks (Fully adjustable 43mm Sachs forks), fully adjustable Ohlins shock (fully adjustable Sachs shock)

BRAKES: Bosch ABS with RLM, Dual 320mm rotors, four-piston radial-Monobloc Brembo calipers, Brembo radial master-cylinder, single 220mm rear rotor, two-piston Brembo caliper

WHEELS & TYRES: Forged aluminium alloy five-split-spoke (cast aluminium three-split spoke), 3.50 x 17in, 6.00 x 17in, 120/70 – 17, 200/55 – 17

DIMENSIONS:
Wheelbase: 1445mm
Seat height: 847mm

INSTRUMENTS: Analogue gauges and digital LCD info display

RIDE
IMPRESSION

T hankfully Misano was dry for the launch, in marked contrast to the launch of the original RSV4 on the same circuit years ago, when the day was rainy and the surface so slippery that half a dozen riders crashed, most through losing the rear end of a bike that didn't have ABS or traction control. That bike was hugely impressive but perhaps the most important step in the Aprilia's development came with the launch of the APRC version, with its superbly effective and confidence-inspiring traction control system.

The RSV4 gained track speed but not outright power with that 2010 update, and was boosted from 180bhp to 184bhp with further tweaks for 2013. Even the original

model felt fast in the rain six years ago, and the Aprilia certainly felt mighty rapid this time round as the claimed 201bhp sent it storming down the kinked back straight with a glorious V4 bark from the stubby silencer by my right boot.

Revs built with thrilling speed as I flicked through the box with the quick-shifter, which slightly surprisingly doesn't work on down-shifts, like those of the S 1000 RR and Ducati's 1299 Panigale. There was heaps of midrange grunt too, so the Aprilia pulled hard even when I exited some turns from around 8000rpm, kicking smoothly and with superbly flawless throttle response for such a powerful bike. The riding modes have been adjusted to give a new Race mode that has

smoother delivery. It does just that but the difference is not dramatic, and some riders might prefer Track mode's slightly increased engine braking.

Handling was as good as you'd expect of such a light, race-developed bike with top quality suspension, though only after the Aprilia mechanics had tweaked the suspension to suit my larger-than-Italian-test-rider sized body. In the first session the bike was far too soft for my height and 87kg weight, and some extra shock preload and more damping at both ends had it handling infinitely better by the third session.

I also got the chance to use Aprilia's V4-MP, the Media Platform that allows the bike to connect to a smart-phone, and for the rider to remotely adjust traction control and wheelie control on a turn-by-turn basis. In the second session the bike hadn't been much fun, sitting down too much at the rear under acceleration, its worn rear Pirelli Supercorsa SP sliding and sending the traction control working too often by the end of the session.

Back in the pits, it was fascinating to use the smart-phone to adjust the the traction control, setting a lower base level, then fine-tuning it for several turns including the long right-hander where the bike had been sliding most. In reality what the RF really needed was a fresh rear tyre, which thankfully it got for my next, much more controlled session. But the ability to adjust the electronics remotely in such precise fashion is a fascinating development with potential to be genuinely useful. One rider found it useful to turn up the wheelie control for the last bend, where his bike's monos had been setting off a weave on the start-finish straight.

My bike initially weaved too but was impressively stable once I'd firmed it up, even feeling rock solid through the super-fast right-hand kink in the back straight. The Aprilia also steered with the superbly agile yet planted and confidence-inspiring feel that I recalled from the previous model, its front end giving massive amounts of feel, at least once I'd added some rebound damping to stop the forks moving as I let off the brake.

The stopper was predictably powerful, the Race ABS working so well that I couldn't feel it working, in contrast to the previous model's less than cutting-edge system. The RS4V doesn't have cornering ABS like the 1299 Panigale, or a linked system like Yamaha's new R1 but it certainly slowed mighty hard. And gripped hard too, at least until that Pirelli got worn.

What even this top-spec RSV4 also doesn't do is follow the S 1000 RR and Panigale with the option of semi-active suspension. As with the lack of cornering ABS, there's a reason for that – Aprilia haven't yet found the system to give a benefit in lap times, so by their strict criteria it doesn't justify inclusion on the bike.

That uncompromising attitude to the RSV4's development won't appeal to every potential buyer, partly because many bikes will spend the majority of their lives on public roads, where the ability to fine-tune suspension at the press of a button could surely be useful. But you have to admire Aprilia for sticking with that pure approach. Especially when it has resulted in a stunningly fast and track-focused machine that will surely be right up at the sharp end in every super-sport comparison test, even in this most competitive of years. **– Roland Brown**

YAMAHA
YZF-R1

ROSSI'S MOTOGP BIKE FOR THE STREETS...

Yamaha's YZF-R1 or just R1 as it is more commonly known, replaced the YZF1000R and was launched in 1998 with the redesign of the Genesis engine that powered the bike, with one of the most notable changes being the implementation of the stacked gearbox, allowing a raised gearbox input shaft, with the output shaft below it. This in turn allowed for a highly compact engine, which was much shorter than its predecessor and allowed for a shorter wheelbase on the bike. The chassis was designed to take advantage of the shorter engine, with an optimised centre of gravity and lengthened swingarm to compensate for the shorter wheelbase, while 41mm KYB forks at a steep fork angle combined with dual 300mm semi-floating rotors and four-piston calipers to provide great handling and control.

2000 would see improvements to the R1 with tweaked styling and better rejetted carb's for better low end and throttle response.

In 2002 the carburettors were updated with vacuum-controlled CV slide carb's, with new cylinder sleeves of a high silicon alloy including magnesium. The frame was also updated with the Deltabox III, of a hydroformed construction and with greatly improved rigidity, while a titanium four-into-two-into-one exhaust was added.

2004 would see dual underseat exhausts added, new radial brakes and master-cylinder on the front end and a Ram-air intake, with frame geometry and weight distribution both revised. A steering damper as standard was also added to combat high speed wobbles.

2006 would see further modifications to prevent instability, with 20mm length added to the swingarm, while a limited edition model was available including Ohlins suspension, forged Marchesini wheels, a slipper clutch

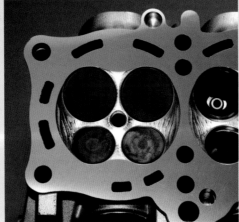

ENGINE

The R1 crankshaft incorporates a lightweight primary coupling balancer subsequently reducing the inertial moment for strong acceleration and consistently high linear torque levels.

The engine is equipped with a 13.0:1 high compression cylinder-head that features reshaped ports together with large intake and exhaust valves of 33mm(IN) and 26.5mm(EX). Valve angle is narrower to achieve a compact pent roof combustion chamber. The engine features titanium fracture-split connecting rods that are 40 per cent lighter than steel. The fracture-split design also ensures that the big end shape has an extremely high level of circular precision.

Forged pistons utilise a box-shaped 'bridge-box' construction on their underside that gives high levels of rigidity combined with low weight.

For the first time in its history, the R1 adopts a rocker arm valve drive mechanism with a lever ratio that gives a higher valve lift than the cam height, while also decreasing the load on the cam for reduced frictional losses. A big 10.5L litre airbox is featured.

The R1 is also equipped with a Yamaha Chip Controlled Throttle (YCC-T) operating a ly developed fuel injection system featuring two-directional 12-hole main injectors that direct their high pressure spray at the back of the intake valves.

Secondary injectors operate at higher engine speeds and deliver their fuel spray from the upper part of the intake funnel. The exhaust system is manufactured mainly from titanium.

The assist and slipper (A&S) clutch has been designed to match the engine's high power and torque delivery and as well as being 19 per cent lighter than the current model's clutch, its diameter is also reduced by seven per cent.

The engine uses a centralised method of delivering oil to each individual big end from the end of the crankshaft, resulting in minimal frictional losses. The lightweight magnesium oil pan uses a sunken bottom design that lowers the surface level of the lubricant.

By inhibiting the interference between the crank web and the oil, this design cuts power losses and contributes towards the R1's high output.

THE R1 MATES A HIGH POWER, HIGH TORQUE ENGINE TO A LIGHTWEIGHT CHASSIS AND WHEELS, WITH INCREDIBLE TECHNOLOGY...

SPECIFICATIONS

Yamaha YZF-R1 (M spec's)

CLAIMED POWER:
147.1kW[200hp]@13500rpm

CLAIMED TORQUE:
112.4Nm[82.9ft-lbs]@11500rpm

WET WEIGHT: 199kg (200kg)

ENGINE: Liquid-cooled, four-stroke, crossplane forward-inclined parallel four-cylinder, four-valve per cylinder, DOHC, 79 x 50.8mm bore x stroke, 998cc, 13.0:1 compression, banking sensitive TCS/SCS, LIF, LCS, QSS, PWR power modes, YCC-I, YCC-T, six-axis IMU, (CCU), magnesium oil pan, titanium four-into-two-into-one exhaust

GEARBOX: Constant mesh, six-speed
CLUTCH: Assist and Slipper clutch, wet, multiple-disc
CHASSIS: Aluminium Deltabox frame, aluminium upward-truss swingarm, magnesium sub-frame, Rake: 24°, Trail: 102mm

SUSPENSION: 43mm KYB fully adjustable telescopic forks, KYB rear shock, (Ohlins Electronic Racing Suspension forks and rear shock)

BRAKES: Banking sensitive Racing ABS, Unified Brake System, dual 320mm front rotors, dual monobloc four-piston calipers, 220mm rear rotor, single-piston pin-slide caliper

WHEELS & TYRES: Cast magnesium 10-spoke wheels, 120/70 – 17 (f), 190/55 – 17 (r) (200/55 ZR17), Bridgestone RS10 (Bridgestone V02 slicks)

DIMENSIONS: Seat height: 855mm (860mm), Overall height: 1150mm, Overall length: 2055mm, Width: 690mm, Wheelbase: 1405mm

INSTRUMENTS: TFT LCD display

2007 saw the next major update, as the original five-valve Genesis layout was abandoned in favour of four-valves per cylinder, while Yamaha Chip Control Intake with variable intake funnel length, and Yamaha Chip Controlled Throttle (fly-by-wire) were also added. A slipper clutch came standard, while the Deltabox frame and swingarm had been updated, with new six-piston front calipers on the 310mm rotors.

2009 would see the new 'big bang' R1, with the cross-plane crankshaft, technology coming directly from the M1 MotoGP machine, with an uneven firing interval and allowing great low end torque combined with four-cylinder top end performance. Switcheable maps were also added to the 2009 model with the D-Mode Throttle Control Valve Mapping feature, which also works with the Yamaha Chip Controlled Throttle response to rider inputs in different conditions.

Other features included a gear indicator, cast magnesium sub-frame, electronic steering damper and revised frame and suspension, including a new rear linkage.

The 2009 R1 would remain largely unchanged except for styling tweaks, until 2012 at which point the bike would also receive traction control, with a special edition Anniversary R1 available to commemorate Yamaha in MotoGP.

The new 2015 R1 and R1M, released this year, boasts a claimed 200hp, with all new styling, a banking sensitive Traction Control and Slide Control System, with LIFt control to prevent front wheel lift, the QSS quick shift system and all new power modes, as well as ABS. The focus is now on the R1 being a track orientated machine, akin to the MotoGP bikes, with the M providing a track or race ready option, including electronic suspension. Keep reading for full impressions on the new R1.

CHASSIS & STYLING

Featuring gravity cast components that are welded together to form a single structural unit, the compact aluminium main frame offers an ideal balance of strength and rigidity. Weighing in at just 199kg with full oil and fuel and only 179kg dry the R1's racing DNA is evident in the design and construction of every component.

The wheelbase is 10mm shorter and the 570mm swingarm is 15mm shorter. Both the caster and fork offset are the same as the current R1 and axle diameter is increased by 3mm to 25mm.

The suspension has been developed by KYB in association with Yamaha. The 43mm forks give 120mm of travel. At the rear end, the ly designed upward-truss swingarm activates a link-type Monocross system.

The R1 is equipped with ABS and also Yamaha's Unified Brake System.

With the Unified Brake System, operation of the front brake also generates a corresponding braking force at the rear and when the rider operates both the front and rear brakes, the Unified Brake System controls the balance of braking force that is applied to each brake.

The cast magnesium wheels represent a weight saving of nearly 900g. The 17-litre aluminium fuel tank weighs 1.6kg less than an equivalent steel design.

By using aerodynamic analysis to create a more efficient shape, Yamaha's designers have succeeded in producing a cowl and screen that deliver a reduction of eight per cent in wind resistance. In a further move to achieve a low overall weight, Yamaha's designers have chosen to equip the R1

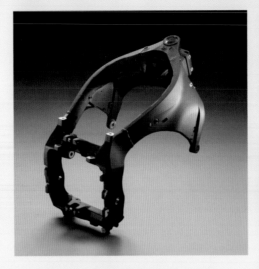

with LED headlights and LED position lights.

The body design of the R1 has been shaped by the demands of the racetrack, and for this reason Yamaha used their winning MotoGP M1 as inspiration.

One of the most revolutionary design features on the R1 is its radical face with a unique 'headlight-less' look. In place of the usual twin headlights, this front cowl is equipped with thin and straight LED position lights, while the compact LED headlights are located within the leading edge of the side cowling.

ELECTRONICS

The R1 is equipped with a highly sophisticated 6-axis Inertial Measurement Unit (IMU) that instantaneously delivers comprehensive machine running data to the ECU.

Developed exclusively for the R1, this six-axis IMU consists of three gyro sensors that measures machine pitch, roll and yaw, as well as three G-sensors that transmit data on forward/backward, left/right and up/down acceleration. By constantly analysing this data, the IMU is able to establish the R1's position and behaviour – including lean angle, slide speed and pitching rate. Data is then sent via a CAN system to the ECU that makes real time calculations and instantly adjusts the R1's various electronic control systems in order to achieve optimum performance with high levels of controllability.

This in turn has enabled Yamaha to equip this superbike with the most advanced MotoGP technology, such as a banking angle sensitive rear wheel Slide Control System (SCS) and Traction Control System (TCS).

TCS is able to optimise the drive force to the rear tyre by monitoring the difference in speed between the front and rear wheels, and if it detects that rear wheel traction is being lost, the ECU adjusts the throttle valve opening, fuelling and ignition timing accordingly.

The R1's ly developed TCS takes the concept to the next level by using additional data relating to the bike's banking angle when calculating the optimum rear wheel control settings. For example, when the R1 is cornering at a high banking angle, the IMU's sensors will activate the TCS to a higher level of control than when the motorcycle is upright allowing the R1 rider to achieve optimum performance on a circuit, or whether powering out of a corner or accelerating in a straight line.

Yamaha's patented Slide Control System (SCS) is designed to limit sidewards movement of the rear tyre by adjusting the

engine's output to an optimal level via the ECU when a slide is detected.

The third weapon in the R1's control armory is its LIFt control system (LIF) that has been developed to control front wheel lift when accelerating hard.

For fast, smooth and efficient starts, the Launch Control System (LCS) restricts engine rpm to below 10,000rpm even at full throttle. This control system also uses information from the TCS and LIF systems in order to maintain an optimum level of engine output when accelerating away from the start line, allowing the rider to concentrate fully on the crucial first few seconds of any race. The Quick Shift System (QSS) gives seamless upshifts.

The ly developed Power mode selection (PWR) gives the option to choose from a selection of four different adjustable running modes.

The YRC offers four grouped presets for quick and simple 'one-click' selection of all electronic controls through easy handlebar switches. In the (YRC) each of the control modes can be freely adjusted into combinations based on user preferences and riding environment.

With its wide array of electronic controls, the R1 produces a mass of information and Yamaha have developed an effective rider-machine interface that conveys the data in a clear and intuitive manner.

The dash can be set to either 'Street' or 'Track' mode with a choice of a black or white background. In 'Street' mode the display features items such as gear position, while the tachometer bar display uses different colours as the revs increase, allowing the rider to instantly comprehend the data. Other items available in 'Street' mode include odometer, tripmeters, real-time fuel efficiency, average fuel efficiency and amount of fuel consumed.

In 'Track' mode the display shows specific information with a high degree of clarity, such as lap number, lap times and a stopwatch function. The bar type tachometer display starts at 8000rpm and runs to the red line, and the gear position indicator is prominently displayed to the right of the panel.

The R1M features Ohlins Electronic Racing Suspension, full carbon-fibre bodywork and the Communication Control Unit (CCU) which records a wide range of running data.

RIDE IMPRESSION

I fire the bike up with the starter button/kill switch, select first gear and roll out of pit lane. I've been riding here for 20-years so that means I am lucky enough to be able to focus on the test rather than which way the track goes.

After the sighting laps it is go time and as I run onto the front chute I twist that YCC-T throttle wide open for the first time. The R1's acceleration is stunning – the LIF wheelie control stopping the bike getting too high. Seat of the pants dyno it feels like a genuine 185-190-rear-wheel-horsepower motorcycle (note: we were told our bikes ran the Track ECU - not speed limited and no linked brakes). But it is not the power that impresses and thrills, it is the rapid acceleration

that really stands out and above 11,000rpm the bike keeps revving like mad!

Thanks to high compression, a lightweight crankshaft, titanium conrods, lightweight pistons and a conrod ratio that promotes acceleration this engine revs fast. For a non-pressurized (turbo or supercharged) engine it is amazing how much air it gulps!

The gearbox action via the quickshifter is swift and positive and progress forward comes at a rapid rate not unlike that of a real world superbike. In fact, my vote is this is the fastest accelerating production litre-class bike yet. I'm yet to ride the S 1000 RR, RSV-4 or 1299 Duke though.

The bottom-end punch of the older model has

gone but the mid-range and top end is incredible. The slipper clutch is brilliant and the bike runs into turns like a two-stroke.

I tried the TCS, SCS, PWR and LIF on 3 across the board for my first session – this was too intrusive so was reduced to 2 across the board, then 1 across the board. I finally settled on 1 for TCS, 1 for SCS, LIF switched off and PWR set to 2, as the throttle was smoother on 2. I did not have time to test launch control, QSS settings or YRC presets. I needed another full day or two to fully explore this – and this test was purely a six-session sample for us journalists.

There were some aspects of the YCC-T that I felt could be improved as I felt I did not have a connection between my throttle hand and the

back tyre – the very thing Yamaha engineered into this bike – but can't judge that fully until I have more time to play with settings to get the throttle/ride connection more natural feeling to give that rider control back. The rest of the rider aids were first class. The TCS very smooth and I did not notice the SCS directly but I do know the rear tyres were really wrecked by the final session and the bike was very loose – however, it just moves around but does not crash.

The anti-wheelie I preferred not to use.

Handling was never a strong point for the outgoing R1, which was heavy and bulky with a heavy crank and engine that was low and forward. Not so now...

Steering is fast and accurate on initial turn, the front-end feel is confidence inspiring on the brakes into turns and the bike hooks up and drives off corners incredibly well. Mid-corner the stock standard out of the crate suspension settings were very soft for my 94kg and experience level, not doing the bike any favours but we adjusted that out quite a lot

with simple preload and compression and the cornering performance improved.

I would have kept going much firmer had I had more sessions. There was some rear tyre sidewall pump on the gas exiting turns with the RSR10 also. With more time and set-up the potential is there for the bike to be brilliant but with TCS, SCS, LIF, LCS, QSS, PWR and YRC there are endless set-up options and ownership is the only way to explore these.

Braking performance is first rate. Initial bite is strong but very controlled and the lever can be intimately modulated into the turns. I did not feel the ABS at all (Track ECU has a special track ABS setting), however, although the linked brakes were disabled, the rear of the bike would still back into turns on the brakes – without rear brake input from me. More front fork support would help. Easy fix.

Mid-turn corner speed is good but once you crack that throttle make sure you are on line as the bike will fire off with ferocious speed. It's a deep on the brakes, turn and fire off the corner bike for the modern riding style. Short

wheelbase bikes can definitely be fantastic for old school sweeping lines too – as long as the geometry is right – and the R1 is no exception. It just makes more sense to get on the fat part of the tyre and use the amazing engine acceleration and electronics.

Back to the fuel tank size. I use a fuel tank a lot – I place my sternum on the edge of the side of a tank while I corner and brake/corner. I also use my abdominal area to help support myself under brakes and my outside arm to support myself during cornering. These points of contact were not accessible for me on the R1, meaning all of my weight was on the 'bars/my arms. This meant I could not steer smoothly or lock onto the bike and steer with a relaxed upper body. I noticed a lot of the taller riders who were fast also getting tired on the bike for the very same reason I suspect. Tank grips for the knees might help or sliding the 'bars down the forks – but then you have the issue of more weight on the front. Not sure what the fix is there but it is something I have never struck before. Bikes are getting too small!

Aside from that – which would not be an issue on the street – I rate the YZF-R1 a 10/10. It has improved incredibly and set a benchmark of performance and technology. A true MotoGP bike for the customer. The last time Yamaha gave us a true racer for the road was with the OW01 and this R1 certainly makes me feel it's as special as the OW01 was...

YZF-R1M

I rode the YZF-R1M for the afternoon sessions and before I tell you how amazing it was, I should explain what you get for $29,990 + ORC.

The YZF-R1M is equipped with an Öhlins Electronic Racing Suspension (ERS) system.

This system takes data from the six-axis IMU and various sensors, and based on the running conditions the system's Suspension Control Unit (SCU) makes integrated adjustments to the front and rear suspension. This Electronic Racing Suspension (ERS) offers a choice of 'Automatic' and 'Manual' modes, and within each of these two modes

THE YZF-R1M IS A GENUINE FACTORY RACER FOR THE STREETS...

there is a selection of three different settings. The design of the ERS also permits the independent adjustment of the compression and rebound damping functions.

As a genuine 'factory racer', the YZF-R1M is equipped with a full carbon fairing, carbon front guard and carbon seat cover. Fitted as standard equipment on the YZF-R1M, the Communication Control Unit (CCU) allows riders to record a wide range of running data, including lap times, speed, throttle position, GPS tracking, lean angle and more. Data can be viewed, compared and shared on a tablet using a wireless connection with the R1's CCU, enabling riders to analyse the previous race or track session and make any necessary adjustments.

So how does the R1M compare to the R1? First of all the extra grip of the Bridgestone V02

slick tyres made a huge difference and makes it difficult to compare to the bike on treaded tyres. The M also had a larger rear sprocket fitted to compensate for the 200-section tyre but still, gearing was much more suited to the track and first gear was not required.

Ergonomically there is no real difference (5mm seat height) on the bikes but the ride experience is very different. The M is fantastic and much more like a set-up racer or track day bike. The automatic mode on the ERS was fine for me and the firmer fork springs made a huge difference to the bike on the brakes. The rear shock is marginally firmer but I still found it soft in the back – easily adjusted.

Obviously the quality Ohlins suspension makes a difference but I would be interested to try the KYB with the same spring rates as the Ohlins to get a true comparison. The M suspension helped bring out the true potential in the R1 chassis and handling and I was definitely able to push much, much harder on the M. – JEFF WARE

SUZUKI GSX-R1000

THE GIXER 1000 IS THE MASTER OF MUSCLEBIKES...

The GSX-R1000 first made an appearance in 2001, replacing Suzuki's flagship sportsbike, the GSX-R1100.

It was a smaller displacement offering, sharing many features with the GSX-R750 including the frame, although on the GSX-R1000 it was manufactured with thicker material for 10 per cent more rigidity to help with the additional power on tap. The engine was also a larger version of the GSX-R750 engine, but with an extra 1mm of bore, and 13mm of stroke.

Other features included new pistons with lower crowns and a gear-driven counter balancer, while titanium exhaust headers and

inner silencer tube helping reduce weight over the system used on the 750.

2003 would see an updated GSX-R1000, the K3, with a reinforced aluminium frame featuring internal ribs, while both it and the frame were painted black.

The front brakes were replaced with radially mounted four-piston calipers, with smaller 300mm rotors, that provided better performance than the original six-piston items.

Better performance was also created with ventilation holes between cylinders, equalising crankcase pressure below the pistons, while the ram-air intakes in the front fairing were moved closer to the

ELECTRONICS & STYLING

The GSX-R1000 features the Suzuki Dual Throttle Valve (SDTV) system with two butterfly valves in each throttle-body barrel. The primary valve is controlled by the rider via the twist grip, and the secondary valve is controlled by the ECM. The ECM reads the throttle position, engine speed, and gear position and incrementally adjusts the secondary valve to maximise the intake-charge velocity.

The unique Suzuki Drive Mode Selector (S-DMS) system allows the rider to select from three fuel-injection and ignition-system maps, thereby adjusting power delivery to suit personal preferences.

The dash has a black dial incorporated into the analogue tacho. LCD readouts include an odometer, dual trip meters, reserve trip meter, clock, brightness adjustability, coolant temp, oil warning indicator, drive mode selected, gear position speed, rpm, shift lights and a lap timer.

The fairings overall styling is retained, with overlapping upper and lower sections and large outlets either side of the engine. The graphics now cover more of the surface and the wheels are pinstriped. The trick stacked headlights are retained, as are the integrated mirror indicators. The rear lights are and feature LED stacks that reduce weight.

The seats (both passenger and rider) are high grip leather designed to allow a rider to be more smooth and stable. The seat height remains at 810mm.

ENGINE

Featuring a 999cc four-cylinder powerplant, with a bore and stroke of 74.5mm x 57.3mm, the GSX-R1000 engine has a FEM (finite element method) pistons developed in MotoGP. The process allows lighter pistons with narrower pin bosses, skirt shape, better durability and smoother valve recesses as well as a total weight saving of 11 per cent.

The benefits are more torque, smoother acceleration at low to mid-range and lower fuel consumption. Compression is up from 12.8:1 to 12.9:1. Another big change is the pentagonal cutouts in the crankcases between cylinders.

They are larger in the current generation and the shape allows better flow of the trapped air under the pistons to flow to the rising side faster, reducing pumping losses due to internal crankcase pressure causing resistance to a downward travelling piston. Camshaft profile has been revised, too.

The exhaust system creates higher exhaust pressure at high rpm so the duration of valve overlap was shortened when both valves are open. The inlet cam was carried over from the previous model. Redline remains at 13,500rpm.

The four-into-one exhaust system has been re-introduced to save weight and is tuned for more response in the mid-range and to eliminate the previous flat spot at 6000rpm.

In the cylinder-head, thinner material has been used for the bucket skirts, saving 2.5grams per unit. This allowed Suzuki more freedom to optimise the valve lift curve.

The back-torque limiting clutch is retained as is the gearbox. SRAD (Suzuki Ram Air Direct) air intakes are unchanged as are the throttle-bodies. The dual throttle-valve (SDTV) were a success on the previous model. Each throttle-body contains two ultra fine atomisation 12-hole injectors.

As the rider opens the throttle, or primary butterfly, the ECM reads throttle position, engine speed, gear position, and incrementally adjusts the secondary butterfly to optimise intake charge velocity.

The ECM also uses the secondary butterflies to help limit back-torque into corners by opening slightly.

The PAIR system is retained to help reduce emissions.

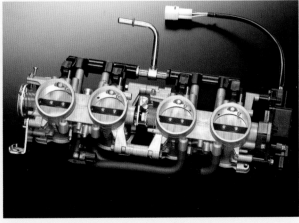

bike's centreline. The ECU was also upgraded to a 32-bit unit, with the entire exhaust now made of titanium for further weight savings.

2005 saw the engine and chassis redesigned, with an additional 11cc of capacity, bringing it up to 999cc, with a new cylinder head featuring larger IN and EX valves, with titanium valves, as well as a smaller combustion chamber with higher compression. The new frame was 41mm shorter with better weight centralisation and without any great effect on the overall wheelbase. Rotors were also larger 310mm items.

In 2007 the bike was updated with a new exhaust system to meet emissions regulations, adding significant weight, with Suzuki revising aerodynamics to try and offset the weight, while a larger throttle-body was also added.

Engine maps were also added, as was a new self-adjusting hydraulic clutch. Engine updates included reshaped, larger IN and EX ports with titanium valves to match, forged aluminium alloy pistons, hollow, more aggressive camshafts, secondary balancer shaft and chrome-moly shotpeend rods.

Chassis changes include an updated aluminium alloy twin-spar frame and more rigid swingarm, with new 43mm DLC coated forks, including both high and low speed compression adjustment on the rear shock, as well as an electronic steering damper.

2009 would see the 'all new' GSX-R1000 with its short-stroke engine, revised chassis and 10kg (claimed) lower weight over the outgoing model. The clutch is returned to a cable item after complaints about the hydraulic equipment previously used, while styling is updated and

assists in making the bike feel thinner thanks to more room for rider's knees under the tank. New Big Piston Forks were also added, to the new twin-spar frame, which is 10mm shorter than the previous model. The swingarm and wheels are lighter than the previous model, with the former longer to increase traction.

The 2012 model would see further improvement on the 2009 GSX-R1000, with the BPF forks revised with shorter length and softer springs, partly due to the bike being 13kg lighter than the 2009 model. Redesigned FEM pistons are lighter and compression is slightly raised, with pentagonal cutouts between cylinders in the crankcase allowing better airflow.

The camshaft profile is also revised and the exhaust was back to a four-into-one item to save weight. Front brakes are now Brembo four-piston radial items, with 310mm rotors, that are thinner to save weight. It is the current generation GSX-R1000, with the GSX-R1000 long recognised as a bike particularly suited to road use, where some of the competition's focus was on the track.

CHASSIS

The chassis retains the basic elements that have contributed to the GSX-R1000 legend: A twin-spar frame that's welded together using just five cast aluminium-alloy sections. An aluminium-alloy swingarm that's welded together using just three castings and is arched to allow the muffler to be tucked in tightly.

A short wheelbase for nimble handling on the racetrack. And a long swingarm that enhances traction and acceleration out of racetrack corners while resisting rear suspension squat.

Although the frame remains unchanged, the chassis has been tweaked for improvements from 2012. The front callipers are upgraded to Brembo radial-mount four-piston monoblock units. They are lighter, more rigid than bolt-together callipers, offering better feel. The 310mm rotors are now 0.5mm thinner and produced by Sunstar Engineering.

The master-cylinder from the previous model is retained, as is the rear brake system, comprising of a single-piston Nissin calliper and 220mm rotor.

The BPF forks are retained for 2012 but changes include a reduction of 7mm in overall length, 5mm in stroke and a softer set-up due to the reduction of weight mainly thanks

A SHORT WHEELBASE, LONG SWINGARM AND BIG PISTON FORKS PROVIDE CONFIDENCE AND FEEL...

to the exhaust system. The softer settings improve shock absorption early in the stroke to help improve grip. The rear suspension is a four-way adjustable Showa shock.

The electronically controlled steering damper is retained and uses the ECM to monitor motorcycle speed and adjusts itself for lighter steering at slower speeds, and delivers more damping force at racetrack and highway speeds, as are the adjustable rearsets, handlebars and controls. A front axle is 38.9grams lighter than previous and has a threaded nut rather than a bolt as per previous models.

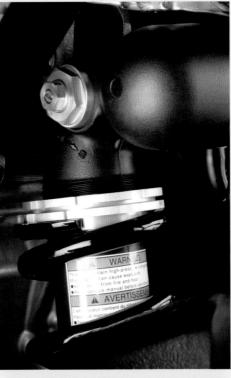

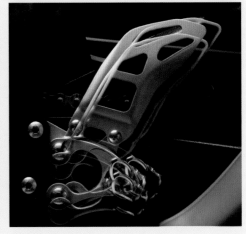

RIDE IMPRESSION

The SX-R1000 feels light, nimble and I didn't touch a clicker all day...

It is so, so easy to flick the bike from full lean to full lean even through fast sections like the Hayshed at Phillip Island. In fact, the GSX-R is more nimble than the Blade and S 1000 RR through here.

The second standout for me in my first session is the fantastic improvement in the front brakes on the current model – a previous thorn in the GSX-Rs side. Initial bite is great, followed by easy modulation through small braking inputs and much more intimate feel at the lever.

Despite the BTL clutch being retained, the bike seems to run into corners more freely, despite the increase in compression. So overall the combined braking package is, thanks partly to the stability of the BPF forks – sensational.

As I get into a rhythm on the 1000 I am also impressed by drive and acceleration off turns from low to mid range rpm. Out of turn four and MG the GSX-R stonks even more than it used to. Definitely cementing it once again as the King of stomp...

One problem I am experiencing and, as it turns out, three other journalists also, is that my left thumb is flicking the Drive Mode switch, meaning the bike switches from C to A to B to C to A constantly throughout the lap and a few near highsides result when power suddenly comes in. It's located below the left switchblock and honestly, for all the brilliant engineering that comes out of Suzuki, I'm stunned that this switch got through.

If I owned one of these, I'd disable the switch ASAP and find an alternative. In fact, I really don't see the need for the three modes at all.

A is fine at all times and the bike is so predictable that wet weather riding is not going to be difficult, negating the need for any map changes.

Back in the pits the lads tape up my bike's drive mode switch and apart from getting my gearlever raised a bit, no more changes are required for the day. A first for me on a stock bike.

The next four sessions are fantastic.

We normally get four but I manage five somehow. The thing I love about the GSX-R1000 is the feedback from the chassis and the grunty, ballsy engine and the 2012 model has retained those traits. The softer suspension, although I am yet to try the bike on road, feels like it could be a near perfect compromise between track and street and along with the chassis feedback, the bike promotes confidence in the rider and this was really highlighted by the fact that I could spin and slide the rear tyre off some of the faster corners with confidence – not my usual style.

I'm no ex dirt tracker, no way. I also had a few front tucks midway through turn two and I was able to easily ride them out. These things highlight what a brilliant chassis the bike has – and with more track oriented rubber it would have been on rails.

The GSX-R is a fantastic bike for those of us who need feedback and feel and didn't grow up riding GP bikes with stiff chassis'. All of that feel translates to a good roadbike and no wonder the Gixer has always been a favourite on Aussie roads. So much information is available from the pegs, the seat, the bars and generally the bike just moving around nicely.

It's a brilliantly communicable machine in an era where stiffness is taking feel away from us riders and then electronics are being dialled in to compensate. The lap time goes down but the riding experience often does also. With the Suzuki, I still get that proper riding experience buzz. I feel like I'm the one in control...

The engine characteristics perfectly compliment the chassis. High performance with predictability and lots and lots of feel on the throttle. For me, it is a real bonus. I like my right wrist and brain to be a directly linked to that back wheel as possible and the GSX-R is fantastic in that area. Feeding power on predictable and finding grip is easy and the bike doesn't need traction control. The smooth engine and the ECU controlled secondary butterflies take care of all that, along with the conrod ratio, cam profiles and power curve, and allow the rider to be the traction control.

Sure, as big horsepower numbers slowly out grow the current street sportsbike tyres, TC is handy, but not necessary on all bikes.

Like the GSX-R600, the 1000 to feels, to

"THE GSX-R STONKS EVEN MORE THAN IT USED TO... DEFINITELY CEMENTING IT ONCE AGAIN AS THE KING OF STOMP..."

me, like the most compact bike in class, and I find that difficult. I had to lower the pegs and I only just fit in the bike. I can ride it comfortably but found it difficult to keep my feet and legs in tight. I hope they don't get any smaller in the future.

In terms of technology the GSX-R1000 doesn't tick all the boxes but if you do your homework you will actually see that there is a hell of a lot of technology in the hardware that makes up this machine. The incredible 27 years of R&D Suzuki have with the GSX-R range is invaluable and immeasurable. Yet they have somehow managed to keep that GSX-R mojo in there. I have a 1985 model and I could feel that bike in the new model while I lapped Phillip Island. Just magic...
– JEFF WARE

SPECIFICATIONS
SUZUKI GSX-R1000

CLAIMED POWER: 136kW[184hp]@11500rpm
CLAIMED TORQUE: 117Nm[84.2ft-lbs]@10000rpm
CLAIMED WEIGHT: 203kg

ENGINE: Liquid-cooled, DOHC, 16 valve, inline four-cylinder, four-stroke, 74.5 x 57.3mm, 999cc, 12.9:1, EFI

GEARBOX: Six speed.
CLUTCH: Wet multi-plate slipper clutch.
CHASSIS: Twin-spar aluminium, cast aluminium swingarm, Rake: 23.5 degrees, Trail: 98mm

SUSPENSION: Dual inverted 43mm Showa BPF forks, fully adjustable, 118mm travel, Showa monoshock, fully adjustable, 130mm travel

BRAKES: Dual 310mm front rotors, four-piston radial mount Brembo monoblock calipers, single 220mm rotor with single-piston caliper

WHEELS & TYRES: Cast alloy, 3.50 x 17in, 6.00 x 17in, Dunlop SportSmart 120/70 – 17, 190/50 – 17

DIMENSIONS: Seat height: 810mm, Overall width: 1130mm, Overall length: 2045mm, Wheelbase: 1405mm

INSTRUMENTS: Multi-function display

KAWASAKI NINJA ZX-10R

MUTLIPLE WORLD SUPERBIKE TITLES AND YOU CAN HAVE ONE FOR THE STREET...

The Kawasaki ZX-10R replaced the ZX-9R which was Kawasaki's answer to the original Honda Fireblade as a bike that combined the ZXR750's handling with the ZZ-R1100's power but ended up a compromise that didn't quite live up to the competition of the time.

The ZX-10R on the other hand was released in 2004, featuring a narrow chassis with a 998cc inline four-cylinder engine, including a triangular layout for the crankshaft axis, input shaft and output shaft to assist in keeping the engine length to a minimum, while a one-piece cylinder and crankcase assembly helped increase rigidity but also reduced weight. Machined chomoly steel double overhead cams ensured strength, with forged pistons offering a lightweight solution in the ZX-10R's angry engine.

Other inclusions were a slipper clutch as well as new wheels, claimed to be almost as light as racing wheels, while the exhaust was

THE LATEST ZX-10R RECEIVED THE SPORT KAWASAKI TRACTION CONTROL SYSTEM ALONG WITH BIG PISTON FORKS TO MAKE FOR A KILLER PACKAGE...

a full titanium system with single muffler.

With a short wheelbase and lots of power the ZX-10R was a beast and these early models remain renowned as both crazily powerful and quite a handful to ride.

The second generation in 2006 and 2007 saw a much heavier underseat exhaust system, while 2008 would see the ZX-10R return to a single sided exhaust system, with revised and more angular styling.

2010 would likewise see revised styling, with an upgraded Ohlins steering damper and updated transmission.

2011 heralded the latest generation of ZX-10Rs, with the electronics package receiving a major overhaul to include the Kawasaki Intelligent Braking System – or ABS, optionally, while the Sport Kawasaki Traction Control system (S-KTRC) would come as standard.

Other features of note for the 2011-onwards models was redesigned styling, larger throttle-bodies, new lighter wheels, Showa Big Piston Forks, LCD dash, adjustable footpegs and of course all new styling, with an Ohlins electronic steering damper also replacing the previous unit in 2013. Power on the 2011 onwards models is also a claimed 160hp, starting to show the bike's age, although Tom Sykes on board the WSBK Kawasaki only lost out on the 2014 Championship by the narrowest of margins.

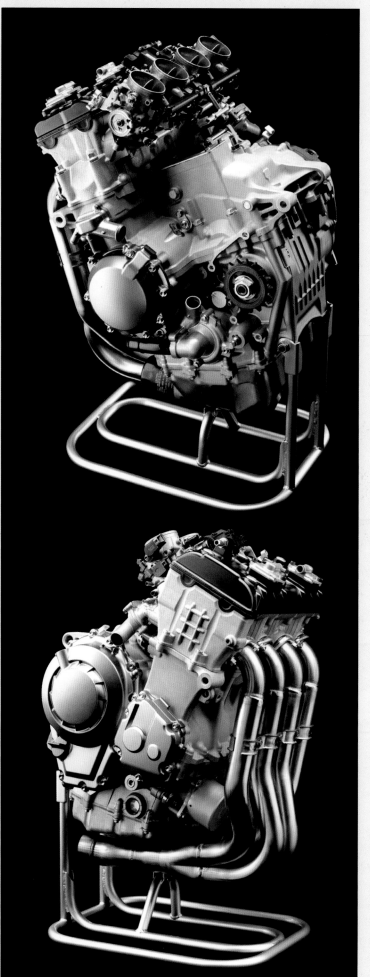

ENGINE

It shouldn't come as a big surprise that the 2011 onwards Ninja has quite a peaky power output. While the capacity's the same as before, the inlet valves are bigger, the valve timing is wilder and there's 0.6mm more valve lift. The airbox is bigger and with a smoother shape to aid the additional air flow too.

But there are many more subtle as well as fundamental changes to the engine. The cylinders for example are now offset relative to the crankshaft. They're shifted by 2mm from the crank's centre line so that on the power stroke the conrod is at less of an angle to the pistons, which in turn means reduced side thrust during this high pressure phase and less friction. Following from that, the pistons experience less force and can be made lighter, reducing the loads on the conrods and crank.

In order to move the bike's main masses as close as possible to the centre of gravity, the crankshaft has been raised in the bike, and because it's higher the gearbox input and output shafts have been flipped – on the bike the input is above the output where they were the other way around before, in order to keep the final drive sprocket in the right position relative to the swingarm pivot.

To compensate for this the fuel tank drops deeper down behind the airbox, so the fuel is carried lower and the overall centre of gravity is 4mm lower than before. It's also nearer to the C of G, helping agility even further.

The exhaust system uses titanium header pipes which have a very large bore size, so much so that Kawasaki claims the length and diameter are almost the same as the race version's. Fitting a full aftermarket system then will gain you little more than simply losing the cat converter pre-chamber and fitting an end can.

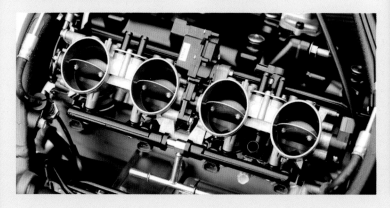

CHASSIS

The chassis has turned more conventional than Kawasaki's favoured semi-monocoques, featuring twin aluminium spars that run as straight as possible between headstock and swingarm pivot. All the sections are cast and there are only seven components welded together, so it's a simple yet effective design which is responsible for the biggest weight saving over the old bike – the new one is 10kg lighter overall.

The geometry is more radical with a half a degree steeper fork angle at 25 degrees and slightly less trail at 107mm, but stability is maintained by the use of Showa Big Piston Forks, first seen on the 2009 ZX-6R, which offer finer and more consistent control. Instead of a damping cartridge like conventional upside down forks. Effectively the whole fork

inner is the cartridge, or damping unit, which means a bigger damping piston, reducing damping fluid speeds and increasing linearity and control, especially at lower suspension speeds such as during initial braking.

Kawasaki's finally moved on from the old Uni-Trak rear suspension design, replacing it on the ZX-10R with what it calls 'horizontal back link', which means the shock is laid almost horizontal above the swingarm, freeing up space lower down for the larger exhaust pre-chamber, which in turn has allowed the use of the smaller and stubbier end silencer.

Placing the shock here keeps it well clear of the heat generated by the exhaust pre-chamber, which thanks to the cat converter gets very hot. It also helps mass centralisation as the shock's weight is further forward.

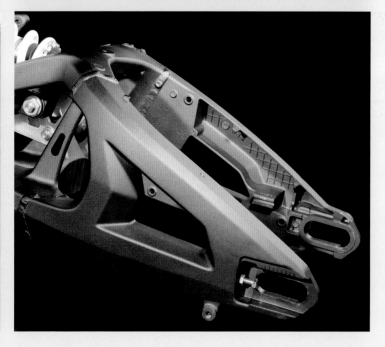

First stop once I got over the initial shock of just how diminutive the ZX-10R was, was the private testing ground.

I rode the bike there from home – a short 20-minute ride, and immediately felt big changes compared to my own ZX-10R from 2008. The latest generation bike feels lower and the tank wider and more bulbous.

The 'bars are flat and low, with quite a long reach down to them, but they are well placed. The 'pegs are too high for me at 185cm on the upper setting but lower is fine (adjustable rearsets). The dash is tiny and complicated and the tacho hard to read. There is a high frequency vibe under 5500rpm that sends my hands and feet numb. The gearing makes the bike feel like a two-stroke in first gear and needs a lot of clutch to get off the line. OK. That's the negative stuff out of the way then...

I arrive at the test area excited. Why? I know the bike is going to impress me and I'll be having a ball on it. Within 10 corners off the freeway and into the twisties on my way here, I know that Kawasaki are back home again – as in they have found their long lost front end.

With the test circuit to myself, I begin to push harder than normally possible on road tyres. I can feel the S-KTRC traction control system working already as I accelerate hard off corners. The rear of the bike slips out an inch or two each time I open the throttle at full lean off corners and then it doesn't go any further. There's no intrusive feel at all, it just stops sliding or spinning. It's amazing. It's like the bike is riding itself for a moment.

With good sticky supersport hoops fitting I doubt I would feel the system at all. I continue lapping and this is a tiring track. I don't want to stop and I'm not tiring. The ZX-10R is silky smooth throughout the rev range. It is fast but there are no surprises.

As we gel together I feel as if the bike is truly an extension of me. I'm not an extension of it. And I put that down to the fabulous chassis geometry that is making me feel like I can place the front wheel exactly where I want it to be from any lean angle, brakes on, brakes off, over bumps, on the gas, off the gas, it's all good and the bike remains composed with no scary stand up effect

on the brakes. It carries rolling speed like a supersport machine and falls on its side absolutely effortlessly. The ZX-10R is almost telepathic. It feels very safe and very planted. Geometry is an incredible thing...

The performance of the Big Piston Forks is stunning. They are plush enough to soak all bumps and prevent any skittery behaviour at full lean or off turns yet as I brake hard for the many hairpins, they cope completely. The bike remains stable and composed even under extremely abrupt, forceful braking. I did not touch a clicker from stock settings during my test – and that is a first on any bike for me.

The unconventional horizontal back-link rear shock was also fine on stock settings, the incredible chassis making easy work of tightening corner exit if the bike did squat and run wide off some hard acceleration exits. But it is so minimal that I don't bother changing a thing. Another first. As far as soaking bumps, rebound is quite fast on the shock however it still packs down over a series of ripple bumps off one particular corner so that has me scratching my head.

SPECIFICATIONS
KAWASAKI NINJA ZX-10R

CLAIMED POWER: 147.1kW [195hp] @13000rpm (154.4kW[204hp] with Ram Air)
CLAIMED TORQUE: 112Nm[82ft-lbs]@11500rpm
CLAIMED WEIGHT: 201kg
FUEL CAPACITY: 17L

ENGINE: Inline four cylinder, liquid cooled, dohc 16-valve, 998cc, 13:1, 76mm x 55mm bore & stroke, EFI with 47mm throttle bodies and oval sub-throttles, TCBI, S-KTRC

GEARBOX: Six-speed
CLUTCH: Wet multi-plate slipper
CHASSIS: Aluminium twin spar, pressed/die-cast composite structure, Rake: 25º, Trail: 107mm

SUSPENSION: 43mm inverted BPF forks, DLC coating, fully adjustable, 120mm travel, Horizontal Back-link rear, fully adjustable, 125mm travel

BRAKES: Dual semi-floating 310mm front petal rotors, radial-mount four-piston Tokico calipers, 220mm rear rotor, single-piston Tokico caliper

WHEELS & TYRES: Cast alloy 3.75 x 17in, 6.0 x 17in, Dunlop SportSmart, 120/70ZR17 and 190/55ZR17

DIMENSIONS:
WHEELBASE: 1425mm, **SEAT HEIGHT:** 815mm
OVERALL HEIGHT: 1115mm
OVERALL LENGTH: 2075mm

INSTRUMENTS: Digital LCD multi-function dash

Not a problem though at fast ride day pace but certainly a rear end feeling on the bike that is unlike feedback from anything else I have sampled in the past.

Despite the Ohlins steering damper cranked up, I get the odd wiggle of the bars over hard accelerating crests, a small trade-off for sensational geometry.

I also spent a day with mates up my local twisties, testing the 2008 ZX-10R with the new model back-to-back and it really highlighted the brilliant steps forward Kawasaki have made.

The new model is smoother, smaller, sharper handling, safer and has better braking performance. OK, the new bike is not as comfy as it's predecessor but that can be tweaked. But the standout improvement is the steering response, stability and the bike's behaviour while leaning into turns. The new model falls in on its side regardless of rider body position – hanging off, sitting upright, pushing down elbows out, whatever you fancy – the new ZX-10R will follow without hesitation.

Bumps do not unsettle the bike and it never moves off line without instructions. Like on the track, feel and feedback from the front end is sensational. An extremely safe feeling motorcycle on the road.

– JEFF WARE

HONDA CBR1000RR FIREBLADE

THE MIGHTY FIREBLADE IS THE MOST FAMOUS JAPANESE SUPERBIKE IN THE WORLD....

The Honda CBR1000RR as we know it today was actually ushered into existence by Tadao Baba in the form of the CBR900RR, first introduced in 1992 and revolutionising the expectations of motorcyclists everywhere, with a wet weight of just 205kg, impressive power and 893cc in-line four-cylinder engine.

It was initially developed to feature a compact 750cc in-line four, however with an eye for road sales in Europe and the US this was later increased in order to obtain 'big bike' torque as well as the same kind of performance offered by 1000cc offerings, albeit with far superior handling.

This engine layout would see the bore increase over its life, as additional power was sought without leaving the 900cc region, eventually reaching 954cc with a bore of 75mm, with wall thickness between cylinders at this point reaching just 6mm.

It wouldn't be until 2004 however that the bike we know today would appear, replacing the CBR954RR to become the seventh generation of RR models, with an almost total redesign over the previous model.

This is partially attributed to the Superbike World Championship allowing 1000cc engines at this point in time, meaning Honda could use the CBR1000RR as a base machine for

their competition bikes, moving away from the VTR1000 SP1/2.

A compact 998cc in-line four engine featured the new dimensions of 75 x 56.6mm, with a cassette-type gearbox, ECU controlled ram air system and butterfly valve, as well as dual stage EFI. A longer swingarm assisted in traction, handling and suspension performance, increasing the wheelbase and necessitating a shorter engine in the new Gravity Die-Cast aluminium frame.

Other features included Unit Pro-Link rear suspension, radial front brakes, an electronic steering damper and much more forward orientated engine for better weight over the front wheel.

The 2006 and 2007 models would see a large list of minor tweaks, while in 2008 the ninth generation RR was introduced in Paris. The 2008 CBR1000RR would feature a redesigned engine, with a higher redline, titanium valves, a larger bore and totally new cylinder-block, crankcase, head configuration and pistons.

Compression was also up to 12.3:1, with a claimed 150+hp on tap, with weight reduction and centralisation getting plenty of attention, including the switch to a MotoGP style side-slung exhaust, lighter frame and new wheels, rotors, battery and brake hoses all helping shed that weight.

A slipper clutch was another addition, while 2009 would see combined ABS become an

option on the newer models, albeit as a safety feature rather than a performance feature, with ABS at the time still being received with scepticism by much of the motorcycling world.

2012 marked the Fireblade's 20th anniversary, with further revisions to the bike, including Showa BPF forks, new wheels, improvements to the ABS system and of course revised styling.

In 2014 we saw the CBR1000RR once again tweaked, for additional power as consumer expectations continued to grow with more bikes nearing the 200hp claimed figure. Ergonomics were also tweaked with a revised seating position for a more aggressive perch and new windscreen, with styling continuing to evolve.

ENGINE

The lightweight and compact, liquid-cooled DOHC inline four-cylinder engine features 76mm bore, a short stroke of 55.1mm and a total displacement of 999cc.

Furthermore, as with the previous model, the cylinder surface is treated with a nickel-silicon carbide (Ni-SiC), ensuring strength and reliability even in extreme regions. Along with remarkable output characteristics, the engine is extremely lightweight.

In addition to adopting the Programmed Dual Sequential Fuel Injection System (PGM-DSFI), cultivated by racing technology, the engine also features a supported material with high adsorbability

for the catalyser in the exhaust pipe and muffler, for a high-output engine with cleaner emissions.

The CBR1000RR is fitted with an assist slipper clutch, of the same type as that loaded in the RCV, making smooth engagement possible. By assisting with clutch capacity at times when even greater transmission capacity is needed for the clutch such as when accelerating, the assist slipper clutch allows smoother shifting and even lighter clutch operation with no need for a powerful clutch spring.

In those instances when excessive back torque from engine braking is generated such as when decelerating, this back torque is reduced, contributing to a decrease in the burden on the rider.

To make a super sports model that is even easier to handle for more fun sports riding, the PGM-DSFI settings were revisited. Specifically, when the throttle starts to open from fully closed in roads conditions such as on winding roads, cornering at low speeds or riding on steep banks, the settings were changed for even greater road-holding feel for the rear tyre.

Thanks to extensive analysis of real situations, the new CBR1000RR achieves particular controllability at a throttle

opening angle of one-quarter or less. Changes in output for different throttle openings have been precisely adjusted, resulting in refined output characteristics and improved throttle operation.

Moreover, for traction performance, changes in output have been set very small in the early stages of throttle operation, and to gradually grow larger when opening the throttle further.

As a result, the engine is able to respond to the rider's intentions, realising easy maneuverability and linear acceleration performance in a variety of conditions.

TO MAKE THE SUPERSPORTS EVEN EASIER TO HANDLE FOR MORE FUN SPORTS RIDING, THE PGM-DSFI SETTINGS WERE REVISITED...

STYLING & ELECTRONICS

Based on key phrases such as "compact, lightweight, mass concentration" that have been notable features of successive generations of CBR-RR, themes of "speed" and "dynamic" have been increasingly integrated into the current CBR to further highlight the machine's racing image.

These qualities of "speed" and "dynamism" have been highlighted further by the use of a wedge-shaped theme and sharp character lines at the front of the bike. With a line-beam headlight and air intake shapes adding even greater sharpness, the new CBR1000RR offers a novel and intrepid front face.

Introducing wind to cool the engine and perform highly-efficient air management, the side cowl and lower cowl that constitute the front cowl have an intricately worked surface shape to allow truly nimble handling. As a power accent on the simple cowl design, the vertical slit inherited from its predecessors

built into the side cowl gives a feeling of tension in the overall styling. And the chin spoiler formed as a single unit on the front cowl allows exquisite airflow control, to improve handling even further.

This cowl has a new layered configuration of an outer cowl with a wide open slit and a rigid inner cowl extending from the bottom to the top. The cowl ensures a large opening to significantly increase a rider's comfort and riding comfort. Cowl weight is reduced, rigidity is ensured, and a dynamic form is created.

Along with adopting full LCD screens offering excellent visibility, the meters have higher functionality from the addition of features like a gear position indicator and a lap timer, for a truly race-inspired image.

Moreover, with a five-level display, the REV indicator linked to a digital tachometer instantly transmits accurate information to the rider.

THEMES OF "SPEED" AND "DYNAMIC" HAVE BEEN INCREASINGLY INTEGRATED INTO THE CURRENT CBR TO FURTHER HIGHLIGHT THE MACHINE'S RACING IMAGE...

CHASSIS

In keeping with the overall aim of improved handling and with the aim of achieving unprecedented levels of riding stability for its class, changes have been made to current specifications such as the damping force characteristics for the front and rear suspension. The result is both even smoother operability and a feeling of effective responsiveness, that underpins improvements in basic riding performance.

The rear suspension continues to use the same Unit Pro-Link suspension system as previous models, which offers excellent road holding capabilities. In addition, the world's first balance-free rear cushion (Balance Free Rear Cushion, made by Showa) has been adopted, and its performance maximised through optimal combination with the unique Unit Pro-Link suspension.

As a result, the CBR1000RR sees significantly improved stability in both damping force and shock-absorbing performance, leading to improved traction. The appearance also contributes to the advanced look of the machine.

Compared with the conventional single-tube structure, the Balance Free Rear Cushion adopted for this machine uses a double-tube structure (damper case and cylinder). The valve-less piston slides inside the cylinder and the oil pushed out passes through a purpose-built separate component to generate damping force.

In a conventional structure, the compression-side damping force is generated in two places with the main and sub damping valves but elimination of the sub valve and concentration in one place allows pressure changes within the cushion to be controlled even more smoothly.

And because there is no small amount of oil being used at high pressures, damping force response is improved and damping force can function smoothly during load input. Moreover, damping force can be generated smoothly when switching from tension to compression due to smooth pressure changes.

With this system, traction and road holding performance is significantly increased. The advanced balance-free rear cushion's control adjuster concentrating damping force, was artfully placed within the Unit Pro-Link swingarm.

The adjuster was placed in the opening area consisting of the seat frame, the pillion step and the swingarm, with a concentrated placement of two adjusters on the tension and compression sides, so that adjustment in line with the rider's preference is even easier.

For the front suspension, the CBR1000RR features telescopic inverted forks with an inner tube diameter

of 43mm and a big piston front fork design (Big Piston Front Fork, made by Showa) is adopted. The pressure-receiving area is larger than in the previous specifications and to generate damping force at low internal pressures, transient characteristics are improved by damping force through such means as smooth operation and reduction of play at the start of the stroke. Combining this with the new rear cushion allows for even greater excellence in handling characteristics and stability during braking.

12-spoke, lightweight aluminum cast wheels were adopted for both the front and rear. Compared with the conventional model, due to the increased number of spokes, rigidity has been further evened out for load received in all directions from the tyre contact points. This change and the changes to the suspension offer improved manoeuvring feel as well.

As in previous machines, the CBR1000RR brake system is the standard with electronically controlled "Combined ABS". In the front the machine is equipped with a combination of a 320 mm-diameter double rotors and four-piston opposing calipers. The calipers are radial-mount, lightweight and highly rigid monoblock type, with lightweight aluminum material adopted for the piston. And although the disc diameter is large, setting the number of floating pins to six allows for reduced weight. As a result, along with realising direct responsiveness, the machine achieves nimble handling.

Furthermore, the rear features a 220 mm-diameter rotor and compact, lightweight single-piston caliper.

For the frame a compact four-piece, aluminum die-cast frame is adopted, achieving both high rigidity and a slim body.

Front and rear suspension that offer more stable damping force, wheels with reassessed rigidity, and a new cowl design mean the new CBR1000RR frame offers nimble handling with quick and superior responsiveness.

THE WORLD'S FIRST BALANCE-FREE REAR CUSHION (MADE BY SHOWA) HAS BEEN ADOPTED... WITH THE UNIQUE UNIT PRO-LINK SUSPENSION...

SPECIFICATIONS
HONDA CBR1000RR

CLAIMED POWER:
131kW[175hp]@12,000rpm
CLAIMED TORQUE:
112Nm[83ft-lbs]@8500rpm
CLAIMED WEIGHT: 200kg (ABS 211kg)
FUEL CAPACITY: 17.5L

ENGINE: Liquid-cooled, DOHC, inline four-cylinder, 76 x 55.1mm, 999.8cc, 12.3:1, Dual stage fuel injection, 46mm throttle bodies, digital ignition

GEARBOX: Six-speed
CLUTCH: Wet multi-plate clutch
CHASSIS: Die cast twin spar aluminium frame, Unit Pro-Link swingarm
Rake: 23.3°, Trail: 96mm

SUSPENSION: 43mm BPF inverted forks, fully adjustable, 120mm travel, Balance Free Rear Cushion Unit Pro-Link monoshock, adjustable high and low speed compression, preload and rebound, 135mm travel

BRAKES: Optional electronic combined-ABS, Dual 320mm front rotors, radial mount, four-piston calipers, 220mm rear rotor, single-piston caliper

WHEELS & TYRES: 12-spoke cast alloy 3.50 x 17in & 6.00 x 17in, 120/70 – 17, 190/50 – 17
DIMENSIONS:
WHEELBASE: 1410mm
SEAT HEIGHT: 820mm
OVERALL HEIGHT: 1135mm
OVERALL LENGTH: 2075mm

INSTRUMENTS: Multi-function LCD display

RIDE IMPRESSION

Predictable, lightweight, comfortable, torquey and linear with a good top end – but now more refined. Stand out points for me on the CBR1000RR Fireblade? First and foremost is the connection with the throttle to the rear tyre.

Mapping of the PGM-DSF1 system has been refined up to 25 per cent throttle with the sole purpose of increasing traction feel for the rider off slower turns and initial throttle opening at full lean.

The result is sensational and truly negates the need for any electronic aids. And the new ram air system that slows air speed at low speed by closing one side also adds to throttle response and torque at low rpm.

In fact, fuel and ignition steps are quite controlled at these throttle positions and

only ramps up as a higher percentage of throttle is initiated – so in real terms the bike has a type of pseudo TC.

It makes driving off turns very predictable and easy from hairpins like Honda to fast turns like turn 11 or 12.

The Diamond Frame Die-Cast four-piece frame remains but has a new rear shock that has two separate chambers separating compression from rebound – which previously involved drilling valve stacks or buying a top spec aftermarket shock. It vastly improves feel and shock action.

The rear getting loose into turns on the brakes is almost eliminated and the same slipper clutch is retained, yet, the PGM-DSF1 settings give the bike a cleaner run into turns – it's a simple matter of back shifting and

letting the clutch out – the ramp type slipper clutches needs to be left un pre-loaded.

If you feel clicking through the lever, you are stopping the clutch doing it's job and the rear will get unstable...

The BPF forks are not new technology but certainly contribute to a greater level of confidence from the Blade.

Initially I preferred the older model front end as the BPF forks felt too topped out too quickly causing the CBR to go offline but once a few tweaks were made to the rebound settings by Team Honda Racing at the launch, I felt the full benefit of the BPF forks.

Initial dive on the brakes is slowed and controlled without compromising high speed compression and the larger pistons – thus larger surface area for the valving – increases

feel and tightens adjustment increments so only a few clicks here or there are needed. The brakes are adequate but still lacking compared to other machines in class.

The gearbox is fantastic. Honda are fairly aggressive on their undercuts to ensure the torquey nature of the CBR engine doesn't cause any jumping out of gears. The result is a slightly firmer shift than some bikes but the surety of a locked gear far outweighs that negative.

The new dash, with six stage shift lights help keep the bike below the 13000rpm redline and in the fat part of the engine and four options on rpm display, plus 99 lap memory and gear position indicator is simply brilliant.

Does it need traction control? Not in my opinion. The rear K3 Interact Metzeler I had did countless laps between myself and

HONDA'S CBR1000RR OR 'FIREBLADE' IS THE MOST FAMOUS JAPANESE IN-LINE FOUR, HAVING REVOLUTIONISED RIDER EXPECTATIONS UPON INTRODUCTION IN 2004...

Andrew Pitt and although it went in the end or towards the end of each session this is Phillip Island and I've never experienced a bike or tyre that didn't lose traction at PI.

The only advantage of TC on the Blade would be for tyre wear and no other reason. You might get a dozen extra good laps out

of a 100 lap old tyre.

The impeccable power delivery and mechanical grip provided by the chassis geometry negate the need for TC.

If you really are wanting it, then for around $2000 you can utilize the existing ECU and fit some sensors and have TuneBoy set up a system similar to the ZX-10R system. Or go HRC ECU. It's not that hard and brings the bike inline with costs of bikes that do have traction control.

I also like the new bodywork with dual-layers for cooling both rider and bike on the side panels, a front spoiler for downforce under acceleration on the front tyre negating that flightyness you experience over the hump on PI front straight.

– JEFF WARE

DUCATI
SUPERLEGGERA

THIS 155KG SUPERBIKE IS DRIPPING IN TITANIUM, MAGNESIUM & CARBON-FIBRE

Producing limited edition models is something Ducati is no stranger to. Every R-spec bike is limited, as well as other models like the Desmosedici RR – the golden goose in the land of limited edition bikes. The Superleggera however, is Ducati's lightest production bike to date and includes an absolute bevy of lightweight materials and electronics, very much in keeping with its name – Super Light. Ducati's model progression in the past 25 years has brought on increasingly sophisticated machines, improving at an exponential rate. Tamburini's 916 is still one of the single

most beautiful bikes in existence and was certainly innovative in it's day. The limited edition Senna version of the 916, built in 1994 to honour the late Ayrton Senna and commission by Claudio Castiglioni, now commands a serious price tag if in good condition.

The ensuing 996 and subsequent 996R brought an increase in horsepower but maintained similar aesthetics. Only 500 of the R-spec version were made and actually used a slightly revised engine of 998cc with a shorter stroke and wider bore, producing 98.5kW at 10,200rpm. The 998 was a further step ahead again and the

final incarnation of the 916 model line. It was also the bike that carried Troy Bayliss to his WSBK crown in 2001, courtesy of the minimum homologation number of 500 units. However, Ducati did produce a 998S FE (final edition) which was not actually a production model and was only available by special order, coming with updated four piston Brembo calipers and Ohlins suspension.

Terblanche's 999 was shunned by many Ducatisti courtesy of its drastically different styling, one of the more obvious things being the conventional swingarm, as opposed to the more recognisable single

ENGINE

The powerplant of the 1199 Panigale was an absolutely revolutionary design for Ducati. The timing belts had finally given way to chains, the clutch was suddenly much more moist and bore almost double the length of the stroke. Some saw it as a travesty but really, it was the beginning of a new era. The new engine lost very few of the trademarks that come with a Ducati superbike. The most obvious one was the clutch grab and sound. The vibration was still there, the engine timing was still there and best of all, the brutish torque remained.

In order to make the bike faster, it either needed to be more powerful or physically lighter. Because the weight reduction also heavily affects the handling, the obvious choice was to reduce weight, rather than increase power. How do you reduce weight from a bike that is already one of the lightest production superbikes on the planet? You source exotic materials and replace the lightweight components with even lighter versions. The thing is dripping in titanium, aluminium, magnesium and carbon, with a few drops of lithium and tungsten for good measure. The magnesium engine covers, sump and valve covers are the first obvious clues the engine is not quite your usual Ducati. Once you get inside, things become even more exotic. Each one of the Desmodromically operated valves, both intake and exhaust, are titanium and 45 per cent lighter than its steel counterpart. The Superleggera-dedicated camshaft is timed via a gear

and chain, running back down to the crank from each head. The pistons are significantly different again – while also being made from titanium, they are the same low-friction, two ring items used by the Ducati WSBK team, weighing in at 194g less than the standard items. The reduced skirt area, single compression and single oil ring contribute to the weight saving and even more so to the decreased friction. The squish area of the combustion chamber has also been slightly modified with a different piston crown in order to increase the engine compression ratio to 13.2:1.

Unsurprisingly, there is yet more exotica with both of the connecting rods being made from titanium. The combination of the lighter pistons and rods reduces inertial mass by 45 per cent over the steel versions which alone is a huge gain for an oversquare engine, allowing it to increase its revs in a much easier fashion and maintain high rpm running for long periods of time. If you consider how fast a piston has to move in order to maintain 10,00rpm, a reduction in mass of 45 per cent of those components makes an enormous difference to the characteristics of that engine. Passing all of the gasses while on song isn't an easy task and to keep that happening, Ducati have replaced

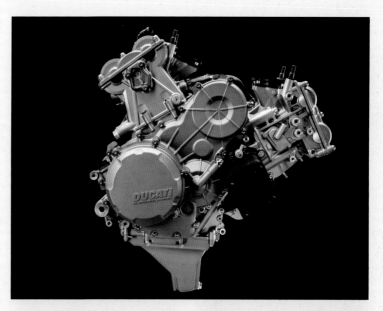

IN ORDER TO MAKE THE BIKE FASTER, IT EITHER NEEDED TO BE MORE POWERFUL OR PHYSICALLY LIGHTER... THE OBVIOUS CHOICE WAS TO REDUCE WEIGHT...

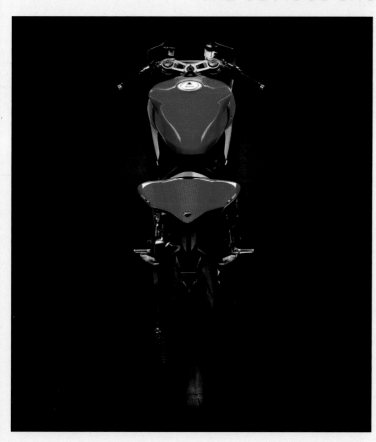

the standard exhaust system with titanium Akrapovic slip-ons and link pipes, weighing in a further 2.5kg lighter.

The crank is even more innovative, employing tungsten as counterweights. Tungsten is extremely dense and requires very little of it in order to balance the crank correctly. This is more of a space saving measure, rather than a weight saving one. However, the crank still weighs in at 396g less than the standard item. While the lower weight is important as it is reducing rotating mass, the size of the crank is also crucial. The smaller the counterweights are (and closer to the centre of the crank), the less force required to turn the crank in the first place, thereby aiding in running continually at high revs as it takes less force to maintain the inertial rotation.

The replacement of belts with chains was not so much a weight saving measure but an extension of service intervals. The chains are also more reliable as they do not stretch or wear in the same way belts do. It is a relatively similar story with the new wet clutch. The dry clutch used on bikes from the 1198 and prior had to be replaced fairly regularly as they wear significantly faster than the wet versions, partially due to increased friction but more often than not, grit and other

undesirable objects often made their way inside open clutch covers, forcing earlier replacements again. However, there is something to be said for a dry clutch – the rattle at idle or the shrill clanging whenever you pull on the clutch lever. Ducati dry clutches were notoriously grabby rather than slipping enough to settle into gear. The introduction of a wet clutch solved that issue (with the exception of filling the aural void), making the operation of it much smoother and the service life infinitely longer. It is also aided in the addition of a slipper clutch to the 1199 models.

HOW? YOU SOURCE EXOTIC MATERIALS AND REPLACE THE LIGHTWEIGHT COMPONENTS WITH EVEN LIGHTER VERSIONS...

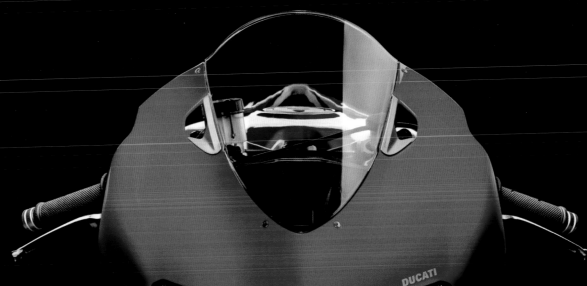

SPECIFICATIONS
DUCATI SUPERLEGGERA

COLOURS: Red
CLAIMED POWER:
149kW[205hp]@11,500rpm
CLAIMED TORQUE:
134Nm[99ft-lbs]@10,200rpm
WET WEIGHT: 177kg
FUEL CAPACITY: 17L

ENGINE: Liquid-cooled, L-twin, Desmodromic, four titanium valves per cylinder, titanium con-rods, 1198cc, 112 x 60.8 bore x stroke, 13.2:1 compression, Mitsubishi EFI, elliptical throttle-bodies, two injectors per cylinder, RbW, DDA+, DTC, DQS, DWC, LIB, Riding Modes, two-into-one-into-two titanium exhaust system

CLUTCH: Wet, slipper type, hydraulic actuation
FINAL DRIVE: Chain
CHASSIS: Magnesium alloy monocoque, carbon-fibre sub-frame, aluminium single-sided swingarm
Rake: 24°, Trail: 96mm

SUSPENSION: Ohlins FL916 43mm TIN fully adjustable USD forks, 120mm travel, Ohlins TTX36 rear shock, titanium spring, adjustable linkage, 130mm travel

BRAKES: Bosch 9ME EBC, 330mm front rotors, Brembo M50 radial four-piston calipers, Brembo 19-21 MCS master-cylinder, single 245mm rear rotor, two-piston Brembo caliper

WHEELS & TYRES: Three-spoke forged magnesium wheels, 3.50 x 17in, 6.00 x 17in, 120/70-17, 200/55-17, Pirelli Diablo Supercorsa SP

DIMENSIONS:
WHEELBASE: 1442mm
SEAT HEIGHT: 830mm
OVERALL HEIGHT: 1277mm
OVERALL LENGTH: 2060mm

INSTRUMENTS: Colour TFT display

CHASSIS

THE REAR SUB-FRAME IS LIGHTER AGAIN AS IT IS MADE FROM CARBON-FIBRE...

The chassis of the Superleggera had to follow the lightweight philosophy.

Despite already being a lightweight aluminium monocoque design, Ducati took it one step further by replacing the aluminium frame and front subframe with a magnesium alloy that is a kilo lighter, sand-cast and houses the airbox like the standard version. The rear subframe is lighter yet again as it is made from carbon-fibre.

The strength and rigidity of carbon-fibre is well known and Ducati have taken the step of employing it in part of the Superleggera's frame, saving 1.2kg of sprung mass. However, Ducati have taken quite a few lessons from MotoGP when it comes to chassis development, particularly when and where carbon fibre is a good idea. Maintaining a certain degree of flex in the chassis is an absolute must for the bike to handle in a manageable way and when there is no flex due to the frame being made from something too rigid, like carbon fibre issues are created.

Crucially though, the use of a magnesium alloy does not forgo anything in strength or torsional rigidity and maintains the same amount of chassis flex the aluminium monocoque frame provided.

The electronic suspension installed

on the 1199S is no longer on the Superleggera, replaced by a pair of Ohlins FL916 forks at the front and an Ohlins TTX36 shock on the rear. The upgraded forks are not only lighter than the electronic units, they're also more rigid and have a TiN coating on the sliders.

The billet fork bottoms are much lighter than the cast equivalent, contributing to the 1.4kg weight reduction. Taking the weight reduction up a notch again, even the spring on the TTX shock is made from titanium.

The both ends are fully adjustable, with the TTX unit having both high and low speed damping as well as. Even the swingarm has an adjustable pivot in an effort to allow even further customisation. Short of picking up a set of forks from Dovisioso's GP15, you cannot find a lighter and more rigid pair of forks fitted to any production bike to date.

The calipers remain the same Brembo M50 billet four-piston items found on the R and S 1199 bikes as they are already the pinnacle of publicly available braking performance. The rotors are also Brembo and matched with the up-specced Brembo MCS radial master cylinder, the braking power of the Superleggera is formidable.

The MCS unit allows the ratio to be adjusted between 19mm and 21mm to provide the exact amount of braking power and feel for any rider. On top of that, it also comes with a remote lever span adjuster in order to compensate for pad wear during racing. The brakes are pulling up a pair of extremely light forged magnesium rims – one of the bike's best features.

Every kilo of weight lost below the suspension is worth at least two kilos above it and Ducati have managed to reduce unsprung weight on the wheels by one kilo.

Not to mention the use of a superbike-spec chain, rear sprocket and even titanium axle nuts, losing a further kilo.

ELECTRONICS

The electronics are where things start to get seriously complicated but thankfully, the adjustments are easy to make. To begin with, two-channel ABS is standard fitment, as is the eight-way traction control and engine braking control.

Also included in the package is the new Ducati Wheelie Control (DWC), which is based on a new inertial platform which measures lean angle and pitch. All of the electronic aids can be monitored on the dash of the Superleggera, all of which is also recorded via the Ducati Data Analysis software, which can now also record lean angles. The tricky and incredible part is how the ECU collates all of this data, computes it all with tested algorithms and then makes the appropriate adjustments.

The resultant action will be slightly different for every single type of input. For example, the traction control may be set at level eight with the wheelie control turned right

THE SUPERLEGGERA'S ELECTRONICS PACKAGE IS CUTTING EDGE, WITH RBW, DDA+, DTC, DQS, DWC, LIB, RIDING MODES, AND EBC...

up. The resulting action from the bike when you are at 20° of lean will be different to that if you were at 25° or 30° of lean, before even considering the bike's pitch. The slightest change in any parameter requires a slightly modified response. When all of this works seamlessly and you do not notice any real intrusion while you are riding, the electronics development has been successful. The premise is not to shut things down, merely an aid to allow you to do your thing with a safety net should an error require it.

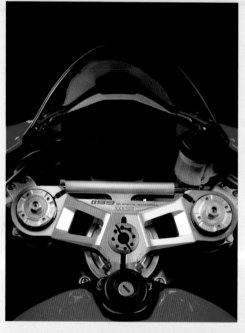

ALMOST EVERY PART OF THE SUPERLEGGERA WAS DESIGNED TO SAVE WEIGHT USING THE MOST EXOTIC AND EXCLUSIVE OF MATERIALS AVAILABLE...

sided version. Performance-wise, it was a big step up from the 998 and the R-spec took Hodgson, Toseland and Bayliss to WSBK championships in 2003, 2004 and 2006 respectively.

This was in part due to a more powerful engine (108kW vs 103kW from the standard 999), significantly more over square engine and higher compression ration. In a return to more traditional styling (and a single sided swingarm), the 1098 was a hit and is already becoming a collector's item.

The crucial difference between the 1098 and 1098R though, was that the R-spec was actually an 1198cc engine, weighed 8kg less, came with an Ohlins TTX rear shock, slipper clutch and conveniently, an extra 15kW. The 1198R was a deviation only in name, employing the same engine specs, suspension and power of the 1098R.

In between the release of the 999 and the 1098, Ducati also produced the Desmosedici RR, the only MotoGP replica bike available for use on public roads. It wasn't just the $100,000 price tag that made it special – it

was the public's one and only chance to own a 90 degree V-Four Ducati.

Fast forward to the 1199, Ducati not only released an R-spec bike but then went on to produce the Superleggera, the basis for which was "because we can".

According to Ducati CEO, Claudio Domenicali, "We asked our engineers to build the best of the best and do everything they ever dreamed of, building this bike for our best customers. Of course, a lot of the things we developed for the Superleggera will in the long term, find their way onto our other new bikes, as well". Ducati have certainly managed that – the Superleggera has the best power to weight ratio of any homologated motorcycle in the world. Ducati's test rider, Alessandro Valia, set a new record for a production road bike

around Mugello with a time of 1:54.9. To put that in perspective, the recent Mugello GP had a fastest race lap of 1:47.654, set by Marquez.

It is fantastic when manufacturers make bikes purely because they can. These bikes are not money-spinners, that is what the cheaper and much higher volume bikes are for. The kind of incredible development and technology produced when manufacturers have the opportunity to make something they could only dream of is great to see, and certainly much more impressive than just developing a one-off concept for a motorcycle show. It proves they have the technology and can make it work on a production motorcycle, even if it is still low volume.

– JAMES PRALIJA

EBR 1190RX
THE BEST, THE FASTEST, THE MOST THRILLING YET POSSIBLY THE LAST BIKE CREATED BY ERIK BUELL...

SPECIFICATIONS
2014 BUELL 1190RX

CLAIMED POWER: 138Kw[185hp]@10600rpm
CLAIMED TORQUE: 137.8Nm[101.6ft-lbs]@8200rpm
CLAIMED WEIGHT: 190.5kg wet
FUEL CAPACITY: 17L

ENGINE: Liquid-cooled, DOHC, 72° V-Twin, four-stroke, four-valve, 106 x 67.5mm bore x stroke, 1191cc, 13.4:1 compression, dry sump, titanium 42mm IN and 35.5mm EX valves, twin 61mm Dell'Orto throttle bodies, EFI – two port, two showerhead injectors, K&N airfilter, two-into-one stainless steel headers, aluminium muffler

GEARBOX: Six speed
CLUTCH: Multi-plate, hydraulic, slipper clutch
CHASSIS: Aluminium Twin-Spar with integral fuel reservoir, optimised stiffness aluminium swingarm Rake: 22.4°, Trail: 96.5mm

SUSPENSION: Showa Big Piston Forks, preload, rebound and compression damping adjustable, Showa single shock without linkage, preload, rebound and compression damping adjustable

BRAKES: 386mm single perimeter front rotor, Nissin eight-piston inside-out caliper, 208mm rear rotor, two-piston Hayes Performance Brakes caliper

WHEELS & TYRES: Cast aluminium alloy, 17 x 3.5, 17 x 6.0, Pirelli Rosso Corsa, 120/70–ZR17, 190/55–ZR17

DIMENSIONS: Wheelbase: 1409mm, Seat height: 826mm, Overall height: 1110mm, Overall length: 2040mm

INSTRUMENTS: Digital display

Buell is a name renowned for innovation and creativity, with Erik Buell starting the Buell Motorcycle Company in 1983 as an ex-Harley-Davidson employee, with Harley-Davidson buying 49 per cent in 1993 and wholly owning Buell by 2003. By 2006 Buell had produced 100,000 motorcycles, but was closed down in 2009 as Harley-Davidson concentrated on its own brand with its stock price dropping dramatically.

Erik Buell launched Erik Buell Racing a month later and produced a race only machine, based on the 1125R and under licence, called the 1190RR. Later a street model called the 1190RS was also released,

with just 100 made and featuring the 1190cc V-twin engine, delivering 175hp. In 2013 Hero MotoCorp, an Indian motorcycle manufacturer bought a 49 per cent stake in EBR, with the two brands to work together, with EBR to assist in development and distribute Hero motorcycles and scooters in the US.

Later in 2013 came the 1190RX, the bike that heralded continuing success for Erik Buell, who had bought the rights and tooling from Rotax for assembling the 1190cc V-twin engine in Wisconsin USA, with the engine receiving updates like Controlled Swirl Induction via the titanium valves to produce an impressive 185hp and 101.6ft-lbs of torque.

Naturally all the expected Buell features are

included, like the fuel stored in the frame, as well as the perimeter front brake, with new innovations such a magnesium sub-frame, no rising-rate linkage between the aluminium swingarm and Showa shock, or the super light hub-less aluminium wheels.

Other standout features included the moulded plastic fairings, that look great and promise to be easy and cheap to replace or the inclusion of traction control, although ABS was not made available due to issues with mating it to the EBR's unusual braking system.

Early models of the 1190RX also suffered from front brake issues due to a problem with the first batch of perimeter rotors on many of the press test bikes.

ENGINE

The Erik Buell Racing 1190RX is powered by a ET-V2 72° V-twin engine, based on a Rotax design, with Erik purchasing the tooling and rights, with the Rotax engine originally powering the Buell 1125R.

Instead of sourcing engines, Erik teamed up with Hero Motocorp for funding in order to produce the EBR motorcycles in Wisconsin in America, with the entire motorcycle produced and assembled in the US. The engine itself was originally developed for the 1190RS, a limited edition race version of the 1190RX, which produced just 175hp.

Further development to upsec the engine to a more impressive and modern output added Controlled Swirl Induction, revised flow chambers and porting, new head design, new forged connecting rods and pistons, and titanium valves – 42mm IN, 35.5mm EX, with dual Dell'Orto 61mm throttle-bodies, while in-house EFI system runs two injectors per cylinder, with a port injector and a showerhead injector in each.

The Controlled Swirl Induction works by opening one of the intake valves slightly before the second, causing the air to rush through and tumble and swirl, improving fuel atomisation and assisting in low down torque and rideability.

The 1191cc engine's compression runs at 13.4:1, with a bore and stroke of 106 x 67.5mm, similar to Ducati's older 1098 setup. The 1190RX produces 185hp

Erik Buell - EBR founder.

however, with 101.6ft-lbs of torque to boot.

The exhaust consists of two-into-one stainless steel headers, with twin mid-pipes, with the upper evacuating exhaust gases, while the lower is a quarter-wave resonator as well as a aluminium muffler, with extremely low emissions according to Erik Buell. A K&N filter also comes fitted to the bike.

A slipper clutch is also featured, and is a vacuum operated item, giving a somewhat unusual feel compared to your regular mechanical slipper clutch.

THE ENGINE WAS ORIGINALLY DEVELOPED FOR THE 1190RS, A LIMITED EDITION RACE VERSION OF THE 1190RX...

CHASSIS

THE EBR 1190RX USES ERIK'S SINGLE PERIMETER MOUNTED BRAKE SYSTEM...

In keeping with Erik Buell's previous motorcycles, the EBR 1190RX uses a number of his preferred technologies, with the first and most obvious being the single perimeter mounted brake rotor, helping minimise weight.

It uses a 386mm perimeter rotor, mated to a Nissin eight-piston inside-out caliper, with a standard 208mm rear rotor and Haynes Performance two-piston rear caliper. Due to using the perimeter front brake ABS was not offered on the 1190RX.

The wheels themselves are also worth a mention being cast aluminium alloy, of a hubless design to further minimise weight. The front wheel only weighs 3.5kg, with a total of 10kg saved over a traditional front wheel setup.

The frame is a aluminium twin-spar item, which true to Buell form includes

an integral fuel reservoir, while the swingarm is an aluminium optimised stiffness item that doesn't hold oil, but does operate without a rising rate linkage, instead using a diagonally mounted Showa shock directly.

The 1190RX also features a steeper rake and less trail than is common, with 22.4° rake, and 96.5mm trail, while wheelbase is 1409mm, which is less extreme than some earlier Buells.

The sub-frame is a magnesium item in comparison, using a lattice design and weighs only one kilogram, with the frame and fuel cell weighing 11.5kg – unfuelled.

Forks are Showa items to match the rear shock, but are Big Piston Forks, with preload, rebound, and compression adjustability.

Claimed wet weight fully fuelled is just 190.5kg.

In 2014 EBR announced the naked version of the 1190RX, the 1190SX – a no holes barred nakedbike version, with all the performance of the RX but even lighter than the RS's 190kg wet weight.

2014 also saw EBR enter the WSBK Championship, with Geoff May and Aaron Yates riding the 1190RX, while Larry Pegram, a wild card entry at Laguna Seca, finished 14th in Race 2 to become the first on board a American OEM to earn championship points.

In 2015 the Team Hero EBR team entered two riders – Larry Pegram and Niccolo Canepa in WSBK.

With EBR seemingly doing well, although still struggling to make an impact in WSBK, it came as a shock when Erik Buell announced the company was entering receivership and seeking bankruptcy protection.

In a statement Erik Buell said, "We thought we had secured funding, but in the end, we were not able to get the funding in place. Therefore we need to do the best we can under the circumstances for all parties in interest."

He later addressed the public on social media, adding, "I want you to know that looking ahead my focus is 100 per cent on helping the receiver best maximize the value from EBR to benefit all, and I will make every possible effort to get the new organization to where it can support the dealers and customers first, and then help find investment to get back to full throttle."

STYLING & ELECTRONICS

The EBR 1190RX's styling is a real standout in the market, with high gloss plastic moulded fairings making up all coloured parts of the bike and promising a much more reasonable repair bill, with the visible sharp edges being the only downside.

The headlight is powered by a Cree (one of the big names in LED lighting) 2000 lumen unit, which is the limit allowed in the US, while the more fluid nose and fairings proving to stand the bike out further, in the three available colours of red, yellow and black.

The TFT display is sourced from a local American manufacturer, offering a full colour display.

As mentioned the 1190RX is light on rider aides, with no ABS or wheelie control offered. It does offer a 21-mode traction control system that can be controlled through the TFT screen and can also be switched off.

RIDE IMPRESSION

ON THE TRACK

I've ridden each generation of Buells and I've been busting to try the EBR flagship 1190RX. There was no official world launch for this model, with EBR being a relatively small manufacturer despite very ambitious goals!

After spending some time setting the bike up for the track I was able to put in a solid 30-laps for my track impression.

The bike was way too soft on stock settings so once dialled it in, with the help of Peter Goddard, the EBR was transformed.

Firstly, the engine is a cracker. Fuelling is very smooth, although the bike was running lean, and throttle pickup seamless and very confidence inspiring. From 6000rpm the twin makes really good strong power, pulling all the way to redline. There is monster torque on tap from 4000rpm but on track, what really impresses is the acceleration rate. No trouble passing 1000s and, keeping the front wheel on the deck was a real job – lots of rear brake over the many crests at Sydney Motorsport Park.

I found it too hard to read the speed at the end of the chute but it felt around the 260km/h mark and off turn two to turn three the EBR is very rapid – up there with the Panigale S.

The gearbox is silky smooth. I found first gear too short and second gear tall in the hairpins. The clutch action is way too heavy, only using it on downshifts still gave me arm pump badly after eight laps. The bike also needs a quickshifter.

Electronics? The traction control is certainly good and very user-friendly to adjust. I settled on level 2 and found this just right. The only three places on the track I was relying on TC was the exit of the old turn nine, exit of the new U-turn hairpin and the exit of turn two before tipping into three. The bike would still gently drift out at the back. It was just right on level 2.

In all honesty though you could switch it off and with that silky smooth throttle and power delivery you would not highside this bike. It's more of a drive thing than a safety requirement.

The chassis? Sensational steering. This is the only bike over 1000cc I've ridden that can use any line at will and still carry speed. No chance of running wide on the EBR – in fact many turns that I go right to the paint on exit I was mid track on the EBR yet carrying great corner speed. Initial turn-in is rapid and reminds me of my old 250 days. Once on its side the bike is dead stable and holds a line with confidence. On exit hard on the gas it hooks up and hold its line. Really good.

Stability on the brakes is not as good as its competitors and it feels like only a longer wheelbase would fix that or much firmer front springs – or both. Turn-in hard on the brakes is confidence inspiring with good feel and feedback from the front and we all know without that there is no point putting the leathers on!

The shock was giving fade at the end and if I bought an EBR for track days I would upgrade to a better shock, as the stock item is not the highest quality unit out there.

With the radical front brake, we have had some issues, and suffered some fade and overheating. When the brakes were in optimum temperature with full lever they were great but lost 30 per cent after half a dozen laps. Our rotor seemed to lack any float and the importers at Urban Moto Imports were in talks with Erik Buell about this.

I did, however, spend the time on a stretch of road to try and duplicate brake fade by doing multiple hard braking from various speeds and could not get the brakes to fade.

Aside from these tiny hiccups, the EBR 1190RX definitely lives up to the hype on the track and is one of the most raceable (manoeuvrable) superbike class bikes I've ridden.
– Jeff Ware

BMW HP4
THE CLOSEST THING TO A WORLD SUPERBIKE FOR THE STREETS...

t all started with the BMW S 1000 RR, a bike produced to compete in the WSBK Championship in 2009, with 1000 models being made to meet homologation requirements.

It was a bold move by BMW, in entering the sportsbike category as a manufacturer whose background had in more recent times been focused on other areas.

Three years of development had gone into the S 1000 RR

however and the bike would prove competitive in WSBK, managing a fifth place in the hands of Troy Corser, while Rubén Xaus would take a seventh place.

In 2010 Ayrton Badovini would win all but one race of the season in the Superstock 1000 category on board his S 1000 RR, while in 2012 Marco Melandri would take the bike to its first WSBK race win at round two at Donington, with Leon

Haslam following up in second.

Releasing the bike to the public in 2010, it was received very positively, with the bike's technology, power and rideability praised. BMW had raised the benchmark, offering the lightest ABS equipped bike in its class, the most powerful bike in its class, the most sophisticated electronics and much much more.

In 2013 however, BMW would raise that bar even further with the introduction of the BMW HP4, with the HP standing for High Performance and the 4 representing the bike's four-cylinder nature. This was the new flagship model, even lighter than the original S 1000 RR thanks to a plethora of carbon-fibre, along with other modifications, and with the addition of the world's first dynamic suspension system on a motorcycle, with BMW claiming the HP4 to be 'the most advanced production sporting motorcycle ever built.'

Available in strictly limited numbers the HP4 would again do what the S 1000 RR had done at its introduction, in raising the bar to all new heights, with it's own unique and instantly recognisable blue and white livery to suit.

Part of the allure was of course the electronics package, with the DDC (Dynamic Damping Control) suspension being constantly adjusted to suit the riding conditions.

This is however linked into the other electronic systems of the bike, including the ABS, traction control and modes, meaning the whole system works together for optimal performance and safety at all times.

Other features included launch control, a titanium exhaust system, new forged alloy wheels, a Gear Shift Assist Quick Shifter and the ability to upgrade to a competition package for even more bling.

Of course in 2015 BMW have released the new and improved 2015 S 1000 RR, which has in many ways surpassed even the original HP4, providing ever better value but without quite the same level of exclusivity that this limited edition motorcycle has garnered.

BMW CLAIMED THE HP4 TO BE 'THE MOST ADVANCED PRODUCTION SPORTING MOTORCYCLE EVER BUILT,' AT ITS RELEASE...

SPECIFICATIONS
BMW HP4
bmwmotorrad.com.au

CLAIMED POWER: 142kW[190bhp]@13000rpm
CLAIMED TORQUE:
112Nm[83ft-lb]@9750rpm
CLAIMED WET WEIGHT: 199kg

ENGINE: Liquid-cooled, DOHC, inline four-cylinder, 80 x 49.7mm bore x stroke, 999cc, 13:1 compression, DTC, LC, shift assistant, titanium four-into-one exhaust system

GEARBOX: Six speed.
CLUTCH: Wet multi plate.
CHASSIS: Aluminium composite bridge frame, partially self-supporting, aluminium dual-sided swingarm, Rake: 24°, Trail: 98.5mm

SUSPENSION: DDC (Dynamic Damping Control), 46mm USD forks, damping electronically adjustable, spring preload adjustable, 120mm travel, central spring strut, compression and rebound stage electronically adjustable, spring preload hydraulically adjustable 130mm travel

BRAKES: Race ABS with IDM, dual 320mm front rotors, radial monoblock four-piston calipers, 220mm rear rotor, single-piston floating caliper

WHEELS & TYRES: Forged aluminium, 3.50 x 17in, 6.00 x 17in

DIMENSIONS: Wheelbase: 1422.7mm, Seat height: 820mm, Overall width: 826mm, Overall length: 2056mm

INSTRUMENTS: HP4 multi-function display.

CONCEPT

BMW have always been at the forefront of technology, especially with their cars but only a couple years after the launch of the brilliant S 1000 RR, BMW has stepped up to another level with the HP4 (High Performance four-cylinder).

The HP series started in 2005 with the HP2, which used a twin-cylinder boxer motor in the endure GS chassis. Then in 2007 the wild looking HP2 Megamoto went on sale, which was a supermoto style bike with increased Boxer performance and handling. In 2008 came the HP2 Sport, the most powerful Boxer engine ever produced with Ohlin's suspension and super sharp handling. The evolution of the HP series sees the new HP4 with all the electronics

and Race ABS, now being the lightest, most powerful and technologically advanced production motorcycle ever produced – the HP4 weighs in at only 169 kilograms dry and 199 kilograms fuelled up ready to go.

If the HP4 is not enough bling for you, BMW have also done what they call the Competition Package (pictured), this bike has every feature of the normal HP4 but with HP billet brake levers, adjustable billet rearset style foot pegs, metallic blue painted wheels, carbon-fibre lower fairing, carbon-fibre tank cover and carbon-fibre badge carriers as well as the sponsor sticker kit for the full racing effect. Other than that the Competition Package shares everything else with the standard HP4.

ENGINE

The new HP4 has a liquid-cooled four-cylinder in-line engine, which is fundamentally the same as the S 1000 RR with a peak output of 142kW (193hp) at 13000rpm, the engine produces its maximum torque of 112Nm at 9750rpm. The biggest difference is the torque has been increased in the mid-range, making for a more user friendly bike.

With the HP4 in Rain mode, there is now full power output but the torque curve that's available between 2500rpm and 8000rpm is smoother and more docile, with a much softer throttle response.

The HP4's exhaust system is made of full titanium and saves a massive 4.5 kilograms over the previous standard RR model's exhaust. The new exhaust system has an interference pipe between cylinders two and three, a controlled

acoustic valve and a closed-loop catalytic converter. The new exhaust system helps optimise the torque curve in the different map settings along with the ECU.

Another first for the HP4 is it's the first BMW motorcycle to have launch control. In Slick mode, this lets the rider achieve maximum acceleration from a standing start – for example on race starts.

We were lucky enough to watch Glenn Allerton test this out alongside a normal start and it was a visibly faster and more controlled take off.

The computer limits engine torque so as to provide the maximum torque transferrable from the rear wheel when launch control is activated, engine torque is reduced as soon as the system detects front wheel lift – preventing unwanted wheelies when accelerating.

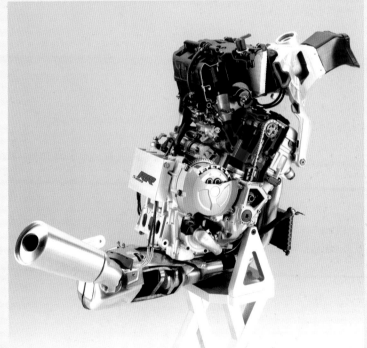

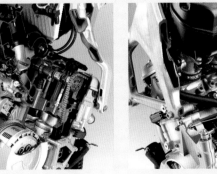

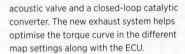

CHASSIS & ELECTRONICS

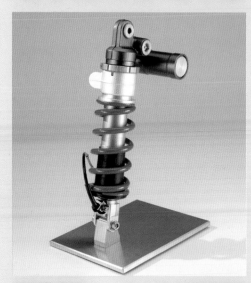

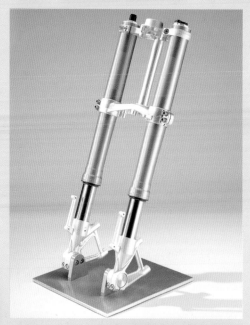

The HP4 shares the same base chassis as the RR model, although the HP4 is an amazing 9 kilograms lighter. The weight reduction is due to forged wheels, lighter sprocket carrier, titanium exhaust system and a lighter battery.

The new seven-spoke wheels are made from light forged alloy and have a new, lighter sprocket carrier – giving the HP4 a weight reduction of 2.4 kilograms over the RR. 2.4 kilograms is a lot of unsprung weight to lose and the steering and handling effects are apparent.

The HP4 also gets a new Brembo monoblock brake system, which uses race ABS with IDM (International German Motorcycle Championship) settings in Slick mode for maximum braking performance.

The DTC (Dynamic Traction Control) which is already used on the RR model now has a new feature on the HP4. In Slick mode, you have the option to adjust the parameters of the DTC, you can adjust +/-7, with the minus having less DTC active on the bike, giving the rider or racer more control. BMW recommend not going below -4, for safety reasons.

DDC (Dynamic Damping Control) – is a world first on a production motorcycle. The electronic system allows the damping to be adapted to your current riding style or road surface in millisecond, by means of the sensor-supplied parameters via electrically controlled regulation valves in the left fork leg and rear shock. The fork and shock have piston rings that are constantly being altered, adjusting the through-flow cross-section for the damper oil. In this way, the HP4 offers optimum damping in every situation, handling long and short shocks virtually perfectly so as to provide maximum traction and safety.

The basic settings of DDC are linked to the modes Rain, Sport, Race and Slick, the set-up menu in the instrument cluster allows the damping to be adapted more closely to the rider's preferences. As with a mechanical setting, it is possible to apply a softer -7 or a tighter +7 set-up. The adjustment of the spring preload is carried out by hand using a 17mm socket.

RIDE IMPRESSION

ON THE ROAD

Like the majority of riders out there, we spend most, if not all our time road riding on some pretty crappy roads and the majority of riders don't know a thing about setting up a bike's suspension to best suit the Aussie conditions.

The BMW HP4 has been fitted with semi-active suspension or DDC (Dynamic Damping Control) as BMW calls it (a world first on a production bike) that adjusts the front and rear damping while you're riding. It doesn't matter whether you are cornering, braking or accelerating, the DDC has it all covered. The DDC is also linked in with the map mode setting you chose – Rain, Sport, Race or Slick, as are the adjustable traction control and ABS – you even get launch control for those mental take offs...

So how does all this technology work in the real world? We hit the roads first to find out.

BMW chose to take us on a 300 kilometre road ride, from Sydney Airport to Wakefield Park and deliberately included some rough roads so

we could sample the HP4s new DDC suspension against the stock S 1000 RR bikes that we also had on hand and I'm glad they did.

Sitting on the bike for the first time is unlike anything I have experienced before, the suspension is absolutely solid – like a surf board, it's not until I turn on the ignition the suspension softens and starts working.

Setting off through the city, the HP4 is much like any other sports bike – not as extreme as some in the ergonomics and has a reasonably light clutch and mirrors that give you rear vision. This bike is not about city riding though and I'd be looking elsewhere if you're planning to use the BMW as a commuter.

No, this bike is all about performance, corners and braking. When we do finally get out of the city and find some nice roads to play on, the rain starts to fall.

200 horsepower and rain would normally send a shiver down my spine and a big yellow streak running up my back but it's not as scary as it sounds – even with the semi slick Pirelli Diablo

Super Corsa SP tyres.

Let me explain why – with the thumb of a button on my right hand controls I select Rain mode, instantly softening the suspension and making the HP4 feel more like a tourer but without the wallowing. This is achieved by the electronics and gyro taking readings from all the sensors and adjusting my suspension 1000 times a second as I ride along my merry way.

Even in the slippery rain on this mountain road, the bike knows how much grip is under my wheels and what lean angle I'm on, only feeding enough power to the back wheel as is needed. Even the anti-lock-brakes are linked into the clever ECU and adjust accordingly to how much grip I have under my wheels to avoid me tucking my front-end and heading bush.

One thing I really do like is zero pulsing on the HP4 front brakes, unlike some of the other bike manufacturer's ABS systems. As I head up the mountain pass at a fast pace I realise I could go even faster if my mind and ability would let me and I watch Cameron Donald rapidly pass me and

disappear into the distance.

Jumping off the standard S 1000 RR onto the HP4 is a real shock, as a road bike the HP4 is just so much better, it's unbelievable – in Rain mode the suspension just soaks up the bumps and ruts and now the road is drying the pace has increased and so has the fun.

Through a long series of bends, I put my head down and get serious with the HP4, the difference over the standard bike when flicking from left to right on change of direction with the nine kilo weight saving is apparent, especially with the super light forged alloy wheels reducing the gyroscopic affect. Even with the lighter weight of the HP4, the bike never skips or chatters over bumps and when I hit the brakes in anger my eyes just about leave their sockets, like some sort of cartoon character. But you would expect this with the new four-piston Brembo

"WHEN I HIT THE BRAKES IN ANGER MY EYES JUST ABOUT LEAVE THEIR SOCKETS, LIKE SOME SORT OF CARTOON CHARACTER..."

monoblock brakes with 320mm rotors and race ABS that adjusts on the fly depending on your chosen map. Even the suspension adjusts itself when hard on the anchors to reduce dive.

All this technology sounds good but more importantly, works even better. The bike just stays on line, even under the heaviest of braking conditions and with the help of the slipper clutch,

you can also smash down a few gears before entering the corner, with no rear wheel lockup – it really is a thing of beauty...

The real fun comes from trying to get some of the 200 horsepower down to the ground while driving out of corners. Depending on the size of your balls, you can select a map to suit your needs but for the road I chose sport, giving me full power with the traction control intervening early, so I don't get spat off the bike.

Even in Sport mode, the acceleration is blistering – scarily in fact. With the quickshifter you can bang up through the gears rapidly and the popping of the shift changes through the titanium exhaust system is addictive to say the least. Hard on the gas the bike doesn't squat as the suspension adjusts and just drives hard while the wheelie controls keeps me heading in the right direction. Gees, I love this bike...

AT THE TRACK

Heading out onto the Wakefield circuit is a bit daunting for two reasons, firstly I'm riding a missile and secondly I've never been to this track before and it's tight and bumpy.

After a few sessions I'm heading up through the map modes and have settled on Race mode. With Race mode the traction control is still keeping me alive but has stiffened the bikes suspension up to a razor sharp track bike – it's like having Jeremy Burgess under my seat, making fine adjustments as I go.

Once I learn my way around the track I start to relax and have some fun, one thing that is hard to master is the brakes. With the race ABS and Brembo monoblock combination, they stop like nothing I've ever ridden before and I find myself over braking and mentally kicking myself that I could have braked later and carried more speed into the corner.

I'm not a racer by any stretch but I can say hand on my heart that this bike is allowing me to ride faster than I could on a normal sportsbike – faster even than the standard S 1000 RR that I did my first session on.

The HP4 feels lighter and steers better than the RR, especially on the change of direction through some of the slower corners. Plus, the increased mid-range torque over the previous model means more drive off the turns and this is even more beneficial for road riding.

We also got the chance to view Glenn Allerton testing the HP4's standard launch control feature – Glenn nails the throttle, which stays at 8000rpm, then drops the clutch and takes off in a rapid fashion with the exact amount of power being fed to the rear wheel for the perfect take off – not sure if the coppers would be too keen if you tried this from traffic lights but it looks cool...

Talking to the racers here they say that you could just about go racing on one of these, straight off the factory floor and watching Cameron Donald do a 101.2 lap on a stock bike was impressive by anyone's standards (I won't tell you what my time was, as I was too scared to look at the clocks).

The biggest surprise for me is the fact that although the HP4 is a better track bike than the standard S 1000 RR, it's also a better and more comfortable road bike.

– TONY WILDING

KTM RC8R

The brand KTM is perhaps most famous for its off-road motorcycles despite strong showing in the Moto3 category of MotoGP, with KTM-Sportmotorcycle AG being the company that continues to this day to produce motorcycles.

The company's history stretches back as far as 1934, however KTM was split into four separate companies, with the motorcycle manufacturing company created in 1992.

Despite a focus on off-road bikes, including a strong presence in racing, KTM has also produced a number of road bikes, including the Duke line, while their 1190 RC8 sportsbike was introduced in 2008.

NOTHING GETS THE BLOOD FLOWING MORE THAN THAT EXCLUSIVE CAPITAL R...

SPECIFICATIONS
KTM RC8R

CLAIMED POWER: 127kW[170.3hp] @10,250rpm
CLAIMED TORQUE: 123Nm[90.7ft-lbs]@8000rpm
CLAIMED WET WEIGHT: 182kg (no fuel)
FUEL CAPACITY:16.5L

ENGINE: LC8 liquid-cooled DOHC eight-valve 75-degree V-twin four-stroke, 105 x 69mm bore x stroke, 1195cc, 13.5:1 compression, dual Mikuni 52mm throttle-bodies, stainless steel underslung two-into-one
GEARBOX: Six speed cassette type gearbox
CLUTCH: Wet multiplate hydraulic actuation
CHASSIS: Powdercoated Chrome-moly trellis frame, adjustable alloy sub-frame, Rake: 23.3 degrees, Trail: 97mm
SUSPENSION: 43mm WP inverted forks with TiN coating, fully adjustable, 120mm travel, WP monoshock, fully adjustable five-way, 120mm travel

BRAKES: 320mm semi-floating front rotors, Brembo monobloc radial-mount calipers, Brembo master-cylinder, Brembo 220mm rear rotor, Brembo caliper

WHEELS & TYRES: Marchesini forged alloy, 3.0 x 17in, 6.0 x 17in, 120/70 – 17, 190/55 – 17, Pirelli Diablo Supercorsa SP

DIMENSIONS:
WHEELBASE: 1425mm
SEAT HEIGHT: 805/825mm
GROUND CLEARANCE: 110mm

INSTRUMENTS: CAN BUS technology, road and track settings, multi function display, speedo, tacho, trip meters, clock, engine and oil temp, average distance, fuel, fuel km, lap time, average seed, top speed, lap top compatible

The original 1190 RC8 was powered by the Super Duke 999cc v-twin engine, but with the capacity increased to 1148cc, with the iconic KTM trellis frame and high-end suspension from WP – a KTM subsidiary. The 2008 model produced a claimed 151hp and 85ft-lbs or torque with a bore and stroke of 103 x 69mm, with compression at 12.5:1.

In 2009 this was further increased to 1195cc, with the RC8 R introduced as the track and race orientate version with a number of improvements over the original RC8. An additional 2mm of bore gave the capacity increase, with compression pushed up to 13.5:1 and 173hp with 90ft-lbs of torque the new claimed figures. Other improvements included titanium intake valves, low-friction DLC coating on the camshaft finger followers, WP 43mm forks with titanium-aluminium-nitride coating, with the same coating on the piston rod of the WP rear shock, with ride height adjustability also offered.

The RC8 R chassis also offered a number of

THE RC8 R WAS KTM'S TRACK AND RACE ORIENTATED OFFERING TAKING THE RC8 TO A WHOLE NEW LEVEL...

areas of adjustment, including the rear brake pedal, handlebars, shifter, footpeg positions, and seat and subframe height, with a adjustable steering damper also added.

Following feedback from the initial release, the 2011 onwards models were revised to include a heavier flywheel and crankshaft in order to reduce the vibrations created by the earlier models, with the throttle butterflies also mapped for better response on small throttle inputs to fix the common issue reported of a choppy throttle. Suspension tweaks to improve performance were also undertaken, while aluminium Marchesini wheels were added to save weight.

A new cylinder-head also incorporated twin spark plugs in each cylinder in order to optimise combustion, particularly at high rpm, with the

second plug only activating past 7000rpm. This also meant the ECU was retuned, with modified cam timing. 2013 also saw the adoption of a slipper clutch.

The KTM RC8 R continues to be available to this day, although more recently it has been joined by KTM's Super Duke 1290 R.

KTM also confirmed they'll be competing in MotoGP in 2017, with an all new MotoGP machine, with early indications that the bike will have a V4 engine but retaining a tubular frame, using WP Suspension and all built by KTM in Austria. Rumour has it they'll be aiming to provide a more reasonably priced machine to riders interested in competing, with their development and support of the Moto3 bikes proving successful.

ENGINE

The dry sump power plant consists of two 75-degree V cylinders, with a bore and stroke of 105 x 69mm, 2mm up in bore size on the RC8. The upgraded four-valve heads have a more compact combustion chamber but the same 42mm in and 34mm EX titanium valves and finger followers. New revised camshafts give greater duration with unchanged lift and have adjustable sprockets as standard – great news for superstock racing!

The waterpump has been redesigned to improve flow to a larger radiator, and power is up 15-horsepower 250rpm higher in the rpm range, with torque up a few ft-lbs also.

Compression is up a full point to 13.5:1 and the 52mm throttle-bodies from the RC8 are

retained. The much talked about gearbox of the RC8 has been refined and a reshaped gearshift star has improved shift.

Due to the bigger forged pistons and revised forged conrods, the twin counterbalancers have been revised and dampen vibes above 8000rpm.

Two throttle tubes are available for the RC8 R – a round track version and oval road progressive version.

There is no slipper clutch standard on the RC8R however the rear hop issue of the RC8 has been addressed with the RC8 R ECU opening the rear cylinder throttle butterfly on run-in, bleeding off vacuum and making the bike fantastic into turns.

CHASSIS & STYLING

KTM employs a chromium-molybdenum trellis frame for the RC8 R, which has been powder coated. The frame weighs a mere 7.5 kilograms in total, up to five kilos less than an alloy twin-spar type and has a rake of 23.3 degrees and trail of 97 millimeters, 5mm more than the RC8.

Front suspension is fully adjustable 43mm up-side-down WP forks with TiN coating, which the RC8 did not have. The dual, 320mm fully floating front rotors are 0.5mm thicker than on the RC8R and squeezed by Brembo radial mount four piston monoblock calipers. The front and rear wheels are forged alloy Marchesini units. Pirelli Diablo Supercorsa 120/70 – 17 and 190/55 – 17 tyres are fitted standard.

Rear suspension is an upgraded adjustable WP monoshock with different internals and a softer 95Nm/mm spring over the RC8 110Nm/mm spring. A ride height eccentric offers 12mm variation, 5mm more than the RC8R. The seat height/sub-frame is adjustable independently of the ride height. The swingarm consists of five parts. Three cast alloy and two sections of layered sheet metal, which have been anodised. The team drew on their experience in MotoGP with Team KR and the end result is a swingarm closely linked to the one used in grand prix. The bars and levers are also adjustable.

There is a 54/46 weight bias on the RC8R. The R also comes with tank sliders, quick release rear axle, quick fit passenger seat and footrest hangers, detachable numberplate hanger and mirrors, racetrack knurled grip footpegs and R graphics. A revised screen adds 5km/h to top speed, a carbon-fibre front guard is fitted also.

RIDE IMPRESSION

TRACK TEST

My first outing on the RC8R was at Eastern Creek Raceway in Sydney. The bike was delivered to me by KTM Australia and set to the recommended track settings – five out for rebound and comp and three out for preload on the forks, 10 clicks out for rear comp, one turn for rear high speed comp, five clicks for rebound and 8mm of spring preload. This equates to approximately 50 per cent firmer on the front and 25 per cent firmer on the rear compared to street settings and worked well with no further changes required at the track on the day.

The bike also had a brand new set of Pirelli Diablo Supercorsa SP tyres – the rear being a 190/55 section, which is standard fitment. Gearing was also standard.

The R looks fast standing still, no doubt about that, but out on the track is the real surprise. Compared to the press bike I rode here last year, the bike is chalk and cheese.

After a few laps to scrub the tyres I get stuck into it. Being 185cm and 90 – plus kilo's means I'm often cramped on the current crop of superbikes. Not so on the RC8R. There is so much room around the bars and tank, plenty of legroom and knee room, it is easy for me to tuck behind the screen and the bike feels very natural. This is important to me – I'm one of those riders

that needs loose leathers and lots of movement to feel confident and limp on a bike to get up to pace. This was instant on the RC8R...

The instant standout is the power increase. The bike pulls from 4000rpm but really hauls from 6500rpm to just over 10,000rpm where the limiter kicks in. The mid range feels stronger than a Ducati and the top end is much closer than it was. As a result, top speed on the long chute at Eastern Creek is up and the bike is much more raceable. The gearbox action is smooth and precise and I had no missed gears whatsoever. The clutch action is light and very controllable. I'm old fashioned and use a lot of clutch slip into turns. Combine

this with the improved ECU control of the rear cylinder butterfly on closed throttle (the ECU opens the rear throttle valve slightly on corner run in to de-vacuum and reduce engine braking – called Engine Braking Moment Compensation), which is extremely effective, and the RC8R is one of the best behaved superbikes into turns I have experienced.

Initial turn-in is still sharp, in fact, the RC8R is more nimble here than the opposition despite the stability of the increase in trail. Turn-in on the brakes is great. The Brembo package offers good feel and reaction to small inputs give good control. Front tyre feel is improved in this situation over the RC8, however, I still don't feel 100 per cent comfortable here. The bike tips in with grace and control but needs slightly more lean angle than other superbikes to carry the same speed through a turn, or to effectively

execute a turn without running wide. It is when on this extreme lean angle that I wanted more front feel. The increase in trail, however, did give me some reassurance that there is a bit more tyre on the track than on the RC8. Ground clearance is not an issue and the bike is very settled and comfortable on its side. It's also a huge buzz to be so cranked over!

Off turns the RC8R is a missile. It loves big sweeping classic lines and with a clear track ahead I found I could really wind the KTM up. I experienced no initial throttle snatch on opening mid turn, although I have read other reports stating some issues, this particular press machine was fuelling well on the track.

At wide-open throttle off corners the rear tyre hooks up and drives well. I experienced no wheelspin or sliding on the bike while circulating in the 1:40 bracket. A slower time on the RC8 in 2008 had it spinning

"OFF TURNS THE RC8R IS A MISSILE. IT LOVES BIG SWEEPING CLASSIC LINES AND WITH A CLEAR TRACK AHEAD..."

everywhere and backing in too.

The RC8R is one of the most stable and competent brakers on the market. From flat in fifth off turn one to first gear turn two, braking extremely hard, the bike did not even get the wheels out of line unless I was playing around with the a bit of rear brake. As a track bike the KTM RC8R is a huge improvement over the original RC8 in 2008. Change the gearing to a lower ratio and it's a true top contender...

ON THE ROAD

Living with the RC8R is easy. The bike is a breeze to wash as there is plenty of access around the fairing. The chain adjustment is easy and quick, so is suspension adjustment. The seat is height adjustable without altering geometry and the bike starts first time every time and security is good.

Like all sportsbikes, the KTM RC8R is at home on the track and needs a few tweaks to make it a comfortable road bike. However, of the current crop of machines the R certainly has the best ergonomics for long haul sports trips and daily riding. The adjustability give scope to all shapes of riders and the roomy nature of the bike, lightweight and narrow layout all contributes to the RC8R being a fantastic streeter. Unless you are a pillion – forget that!

Like on the track, the tall standard gearing needs to be changed. KTM offer a range of sprockets, as do most bike shops, and I would go a fairly radical change. At least one down on the front sprocket. Possibly that plus one up on the rear. This would transform the bike and is inexpensive.

All controls are adjustable and even in standard position fall to hand well. The switchgear is great and there is plenty of adjustability in the lever spans. The dash layout is confusing and I gave up on it. I could not even check my speed easily. Sorry KTM but only my 11-year-old Playstation addicted brother was able to help me understand the dash – and even then I forgot!

Also a lack of gear position indicator is strange – particularly on a wide engine like a big V-twin, where long tall gears can be used – a GPI comes in handy.

I could ride the bike all day – although the fuel capacity is a bit low at 16.5L it was never an issue. Touring was easy and the only fuelling issue with the bike, as it was great on the track, was constant throttle on the road – between 3000 and 4500rpm on constant throttle, the revs would slowly drop away and the bike would slow, requiring me to open the throttle more to compensate.

Vibes are good by V-twin standards. The bike is smooth around town however there is a buzz from 8000rpm or when getting on the throttle hard and loading the bike up. It is never a problem though and is a huge improvement over the last RC8 I rode.

We set the suspension to the recommended street sports settings to begin with, but, the high speed comp was still a bit 'choppy' so we went softer, closer to the KTM recommended 'comfort' set-up. This was fantastic on my local bumpy twisties – you could hit bumps and fire off turns in places that other sportsbikes chatter over corrugations.

On one day of road testing I experienced a lot of rain. The bike was on stock sports settings and was a real handful as it is still quite stiff. On the softer settings, however, the RC8R really is a weapon that would certainly out corner a Ducati in the tight stuff and give the 1000s a run for their money. In average 35ers to 65ers my money would go on the RC8R over the rest...

The styling of the bike is stunning – the amount of fans of the RC8R shocked me and I really hope this turns into sales for the Austrian company so we can see a long future of development for this amazing bike. There are plenty of red V-twins on the road, so, if like me you prefer to be a bit different, then the RC8R is the bike for you... **– JEFF WARE.**

Image: Freeman G